PEOPLES
of
EASTERN ASIA

Taiwan

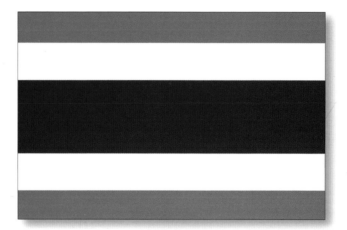

Thailand

Vietnam

PEOPLES

of

EASTERN ASIA

Volume 10
Taiwan–Vietnam

MARSHALL CAVENDISH
NEW YORK • LONDON • SINGAPORE

Marshall Cavendish Corporation
99 White Plains Road
Tarrytown, New York 10591
www.marshallcavendish.com

©2005 Marshall Cavendish Corporation

All rights reserved. No part of this book may be
reproduced or utilized in any form or by any means,
electronic or mechanical, including photocopying,
recording, or by any information storage and retrieval
system, without prior written permission from the
publisher and the copyright holders.

Consultants:
 Emily K. Bloch, Department of South Asian Languages
  and Civilizations, University of Chicago
 Amy Rossabi, MA in Southeast Asian History
 Morris Rossabi, Professor and Senior Research Scholar,
  Columbia University

Contributing authors:
 Fiona Macdonald
 Gillian Stacey
 Philip Steele

Marshall Cavendish
 Editor: Marian Armstrong
 Editorial Director: Paul Bernabeo
 Production Manager: Michael Esposito

Discovery Books
 Managing Editor: Paul Humphrey
 Project Editor: Kate Taylor
 Design Concept: Ian Winton
 Designer: Barry Dwyer
 Cartographer: Stefan Chabluk
 Picture Researcher: Laura Durman

The publishers would like to thank the following for their
permission to reproduce photographs:
 akg-images: 547, 566, 568 (Archives CDA/Guillemot:
 543; Gilles Mermet: 544); Axiom (Jim Holmes: cover);
 CORBIS (Bettmann: 569; Bohemian Nomad
 Picturemakers: 541; Macduff Everton: 577; Stephanie
 Maze: 579 bottom; Kevin R. Morris: 542; Tim Page: 570;
 Steve Raymer: 573; Jacques Torregano: 548); Eye
 Ubiquitous (Bennett Dean: 572; Tim Page: 571; Paul
 Seheult: 553 bottom, 558); Hutchison (David Brinicombe:
 536; Robert Francis: 564, 576; Jeremy Horner: 550 bottom,
 583; R. Ian Lloyd: 530; Christine Pemberton: 534, 538);
 James Davis Travel Photography: 581; David Simson –
 DASPHOTOGB@aol.com: 550 top; Still Pictures (Mark
 Edwards: 557; Elizabeth Kemf: 579 top; Gerard & Margi
 Moss: 562; Dario Novellino: 582; Tim Page: 575; Hartmut
 Schwarzbach: 555; Tekkatho-UNEP: 561); Trip: 532, 540
 (Bruce Fleming: 559; J. Highet: 553 top; Darren Maybury:
 551; S. Reddy: 556 bottom; Helene Rogers: 539; Robin
 Smith: 537; Adina Tovy: 556 top; P. Treanor: 560; Viesti
 Collection: 574)

*(cover) A girl attends a Seven-Five-Three Festival in
Okazaki, Japan.*

Editor's note: Many systems of dating have been used by
different cultures throughout history. *Peoples of Eastern Asia*
uses B.C.E. (Before Common Era) and C.E. (Common Era)
instead of B.C. (Before Christ) and A.D. (Anno Domini, "In
the Year of the Lord").

Library of Congress Cataloging-in-Publication Data

Peoples of Eastern Asia.
  p. cm.
 Includes bibliographical references and index.
 Contents: v. 1. Bangladesh-Brunei -- v. 2. Cambodia-China -- v. 3. China-East Timor --
v. 4. India -- v. 5. Indonesia -- v. 6. Japan-Korea, North -- v. 7. Korea, South-Malaysia --
v. 8. Mongolia-Nepal -- v. 9. Philippines-Sri Lanka -- v. 10. Taiwan-Vietnam.
 ISBN 0-7614-7547-8 (set : alk. paper) -- ISBN 0-7614-7548-6 (v. 1 : alk. paper) --
ISBN 0-7614-7549-4 (v. 2 : alk. paper) -- ISBN 0-7614-7550-8 (v. 3 : alk. paper) --
ISBN 0-7614-7551-6 (v. 4 : alk. paper) -- ISBN 0-7614-7552-4 (v. 5 : alk. paper) --
ISBN 0-7614-7553-2 (v. 6 : alk. paper) -- ISBN 0-7614-7554-0 (v. 7 : alk. paper) --
ISBN 0-7614-7555-9 (v. 8 : alk. paper) -- ISBN 0-7614-7556-7 (v. 9 : alk. paper) --
ISBN 0-7614-7557-5 (v. 10 : alk. paper) -- ISBN 0-7614-7558-3 (v. 11 : index vol. : alk.
paper)
 1. East Asia. 2. Asia, Southeastern. 3. South Asia. 4. Ethnology--East Asia. 5.
Ethnology--Asia, Southeastern. 6. Ethnology--South Asia.

DS511.P457 2004
950--dc22

2003069645

 ISBN 0-7614-7547-8 (set : alk. paper)
 ISBN 0-7614-7557-5 (v. 10 : alk. paper)

Printed in China
09 08 07 06 05 04   6 5 4 3 2 1

Contents

TAIWAN

TAIWAN IS AN ISLAND ON THE WESTERN RIM OF THE PACIFIC OCEAN. The Chinese mainland lies about 95 miles (150 kilometers) across the Taiwan Strait.

Mountains occupy most of the interior of Taiwan, the highest peak being Yü Shan, standing at 13,113 feet (3,997 meters). Most of the population lives on the west of the island, where the highlands descend to a fertile plain. Taiwan also governs a number of islands in the Taiwan Strait. The region lies in a danger zone for earthquakes.

CLIMATE

The weather is hot between May and October and cooler from November to April. Summer is very humid on the plains, building up to heavy monsoon rains between July and September. Tropical storms called taifeng, *or typhoons, are common in September and October. High in the mountains, the weather is generally colder.*

Taipei

Average January temperature: *59˚F (15˚C)*
Average July temperature: *83˚F (28˚C)*
Average annual precipitation: *100 in. (254 cm)*

Taiwan's landscapes include islands, beaches, mountains, plains, rivers, dammed waters, and lakes such as the Sun Moon Lake, seen here in Nan-t'ou county.

Early Taiwan

The island of Taiwan (tie-WAHN) has been settled for at least fifteen thousand years. Some early arrivals were migrants from what is now Malaysia (see MALAYSIA). They took to the hills and were feared for centuries as warriors and headhunters. Other peoples, probably related to the Miao (MYOW) of southern China, farmed on the plains.

Large-scale settlement from China began more than one thousand years ago, when many people of the Hakka (HAH-kuh) ethnic group sailed over to the Pescadores Archipelago and Taiwan. From the 1300s onward other southern Chinese groups also moved to Taiwan.

People from other countries soon set their sights on this island, too. Japan invaded in 1593, but it failed to hold down its conquest. Taiwan, a lawless and often dangerous island, was a haven for pirates.

Ilha Formosa

A more prolonged threat came from Europe. The Portuguese reached Taiwan's north coast in 1590. They called the island Ilha Formosa (IHL-yuh foer-MOE-suh), or beautiful island, and this name was used by the outside world during the centuries that followed. The Dutch arrived in 1624 and the Spanish in 1626.

On the Chinese mainland the ruling Ming dynasty had been overthrown in 1644 by rebels from Manchuria, who founded a new dynasty called the Qing (CHING). Ming forces, led by a pirate called Koxinga or Cheng Ch'eng-kung, continued to resist the Qing for some years. In 1661 Koxinga was forced to withdraw from the mainland and move to Taiwan.

FACTS AND FIGURES

Official name: *Taiwan*

Status: *The People's Republic of China claims Taiwan as one of its provinces. In practice, Taiwan has effectively been an independent state for more than fifty years. This independence is now recognized by many Taiwanese politicians, but it is strongly opposed by the government of The People's Republic of China.*

Capital: *Taipei*

Major towns: *Kao-hsiung, T'ai-chung, T'ai-nan, Pan-ch'iao*

Area: *13,887 square miles (35,967 square kilometers)*

Population: *22,600,000*

Population density: *1,627 per square mile (628 per square kilometer)*

Peoples: *84 percent indigenous Chinese; 14 percent mainland Chinese; 2 percent aboriginal, including Ami, Atayal, Paiwan, Rukai, Puyuma, Bunun, Yami*

Official language: *Standard Chinese, or Mandarin*

Currency: *New Taiwan dollar*

National days: *Republic Day (January 1); National Day (October 10)*

Country's name: *Taiwan, meaning "terraced bay," became the Chinese name for the island in the 1400s.*

Time line:	Earliest surviving artifacts found on Taiwan	Southern Chinese groups move to Taiwan	Portuguese found a port on the island they call Ilha Formosa	Japanese invade Taiwan	Dutch establish a colony on Taiwan
	ca. 13,000 B.C.E.	1300s C.E.	1590	1593	1624

On January 1 Taiwan commemorates the foundation of the first Chinese Republic by Sun Yat-sen in 1912. Sun Yat-sen (see CHINA) is a hero to Nationalist and Communist Chinese.

Koxinga expelled the last Europeans from Taiwan and died the following year. His son, and then his grandson, secured Taiwan as an independent state. Over 100,000 Chinese came to live on the island during the years of their rule. Not until 1684 did the Qing capture Taiwan.

In the 1800s Chinese power and trade were increasingly challenged by the United States, Europe, and Japan. More and more Chinese territory was occupied by foreign powers. The Chinese were forced to open Taiwan's seaports to foreign trade in 1858.

In 1872 some shipwrecked Japanese sailors were killed on Taiwan. Japan used this an excuse to invade the island. They received jurisdiction over the Ryukyu (ree-YOOK-yoo) Islands in 1874, and then, in 1895, gained control over Taiwan as a result of the Sino-Japanese War. The Japanese began to industrialize the island. Thousands of people who resisted their rule were killed. In the 1930s Japan invaded the Chinese mainland, and during World War II (1939–1945), in 1942, it ordered troops into most of Southeast Asia. Japan finally surrendered in 1945, and Taiwan was passed back to China.

Rival Governments

The Chinese mainland was gripped in a civil war between communists and nationalists. They had long been rivals for power but had been forced into an uneasy alliance with each other during the fighting against the Japanese. Now each fought to control the country for themselves.

By 1949 the communists had won and declared China to be a People's Republic. The nationalist leader, Chiang Kai-Shek, or Jiang Jieshi, fled to Taiwan, taking with him the national gold reserves and about

Ming dynasty overthrown by rebels from Manchuria	Qing rulers of China annex Taiwan	Taiwanese ports opened to foreign traders	Taiwan is ceded to the Republic of China	Communists defeat Nationalists in mainland China
1644	**1684**	**1858**	**1945**	**1949**

100,000 supporters of his government, the Republic of China.

Both nationalists and communists claimed to represent the Chinese people, but it was Chiang's government that was recognized by the United States and the United Nations (UN). This was the time of the Cold War, a period of international tension between the United States and communist countries such as the People's Republic of China. The United States agreed to a defense pact with Chiang Kai-Shek and poured aid into Taiwan until 1965.

Chiang Kai-Shek was a ruthless, conservative leader. His supporters formed a ruling elite. They allowed no opposition parties and ruled Taiwan under martial law. However, the island was a runaway economic success, rapidly modernizing and developing its industry.

In 1971 the UN withdrew recognition of Taiwan and admitted the People's Republic of China as a member. The UN General Assembly voted to recognize the People's Republic of China on the grounds that it was the world's largest nation. Taiwan's population was about 15 million at the time, while that of China was already over 800 million. In 1979 the United States also cut its formal ties with Taiwan, wishing to improve its relations with the People's Republic. However, U.S.-Taiwanese friendship remained as strong as ever.

Chiang Kai-Shek died in 1975, and his son, Chiang Ching-kuo, inherited the leadership of the nationalist political party, Kuomintang, governing until his own death in 1988. As the older generation of mainland exiles grew fewer, public opinion

One China?

The People's Republic of China still treats Taiwan as one of its provinces, but the nationalists' dream of a single Chinese nation under their own rule has faded. At the same time a sense of belonging to the island rather than to the larger China has increased. Many Taiwanese believe that their future is as a separate, independent state. However, this could not be achieved without great political risk. Any declaration of independence would be regarded as an extremely hostile act by the People's Republic and is also opposed by the United States. Independence plans are therefore put on hold. A major crisis could occur over the future of Taiwan, and there is a big military buildup on both sides. However, everyday life is less hostile. The two sides do business with each other and are major trading partners. The fact is that communist China is no longer really communist, and nationalist China is no longer really nationalist.

began to change. A Democratic Progressive Party (DPP) was founded in 1986, and martial law was lifted the following year. Democratization continued with a presidential election being held in 1996. It was won by Lee Teng-hui of the Kuomintang (KMT) party. In 2000, however, the DPP's Chen Shui-bian at last wrested power from the KMT.

United States pours aid into Taiwan and agrees to a defense pact	United States recognizes the People's Republic instead of Taiwan	First democratic presidential election	Nationalists lose power on Taiwan for the first time since 1949	Taiwan enters World Trade Organization
1955–1965	1979	1996	2000	2002

First Peoples

The aboriginal people, or Yuanzhumin (yoo-wahn-zhoo-MEEN), of Taiwan are both of Malayan and southern Chinese origin. They make up only 2 percent of the island's population. Communities survive in small villages in the mountainous interior, where they cultivate rice, corn, and a starchy root crop called taro. Craft items are made for the tourist trade. Many aboriginals, however, have now moved to the plains, where they have mingled with the island's Chinese immigrants. Some aboriginal languages may still be heard, and there is a growing interest in these ancient cultures after centuries of oppression.

The Atayal (ah-tah-YAHL) people of the northern and central valleys number about eighty thousand. Their homeland is centered upon what is now the Taroko National Park, but many live farther afield. They are probably of Malayan origin. In the old days, Atayal men and women tattooed their faces and filed their teeth. The women were famous for their spinning and weaving, and colorful costumes are still worn for folk festivals. The men were headhunters, who displayed the heads of their victims in their huts. Homes, sometimes half excavated from the ground, were made of timber and thatch. Villages formed clusters of houses guarded by a watchtower. The Atayal were hunter-gatherers, fishers, and farmers who used the slash-and-burn method of cultivation.

The central mountains are home to a small minority people, the Bunun (boo-NOON). They are noted for their folk song and traditionally remove their front teeth to mark their coming-of-age. Another people, the Tsou (SOO), are former headhunters of the mountains whose numbers have fallen very low. Their dwellings have rounded corners and domed roofs. The Saisyat (SIES-yaht) people are now mostly assimilated into Hakka or Atayal communities.

The Ami (ah-MEE) people are the largest of the aboriginal groups, with a population of about 150,000 living on the mountain slopes and plains of the east coast, many in the city of Hua-lien (HWAH lee-EHN). More traditional Ami villages have populations of between two hundred and a thousand. Once hunters and fishers, the Ami were also rice farmers. Many still farm today, and a highpoint of the year is the harvest festival held in July or August.

An elderly Atayal woman from the Taroko Gorge region shows facial tattooing, a practice that is no longer carried out by Taiwan's native peoples.

It is marked by song and dance, and the wearing of traditional costume. Women's finery includes scarlet tunics with embroidered aprons, beads, and headdresses decorated with tassels and pom-poms.

The Paiwan (pie-WAHN) are a southeastern mountain people, with a population of about eighty thousand. They are famous for their carvings in stone and wood, which often include designs of a snake, which is their totem (or symbol). They are hunters and farmers and fish from the streams and creeks. Every five years the Paiwan hold a festival, called *Maleveq* (MAH-leh-vehk), in which they make offerings to the spirits of their ancestors.

Some eight thousand Rukai (roo-KIE) live in villages in the south-central mountains and lead similar lives to the Paiwan. Many of their houses are built of stone, others of timber or bamboo and thatch. They are carvers, basket makers, and weavers, and the splendid costumes they wear for special occasions, such as weddings, include elaborate feathered headdresses and necklaces of chains and beads.

In the southeast of Taiwan, around the T'ai-tung (tie-DUHNG) Plain, lives another minority of the same size, the Puyuma (PYOO-muh). They are farmers who also fish and hunt. They are divided into clans, each with its own totem spirit. Historically, the Pyuma placed great emphasis on the training of young warriors, and there is much rivalry among villages.

Some four thousand Yami (YAH-mee) live on Lanyü (LAHN-yoo), or Orchid Island, about 40 miles (60 kilometers) to the southeast of Taiwan. The Yami build and decorate magnificent dugout canoes. They live by fishing and farming and are known for their pottery. A traditional Yami home comprises a sunken dwelling and a workshop.

People From China

The many Chinese peoples who settled Taiwan before 1949 are known as Benshengrin (behn-SHEHN-grehn), or "people of the province." They share much the same way of life as each other and make up the great majority of the population. Although all are from China, they speak different Chinese languages and dialects.

The Hakka number more than three million. They mostly live in the northwest and southwest of the island and speak their own Chinese language. Most Hakka live very similar lives to those of other islanders, although their traditional culture still thrives in some villages.

The largest ethnic group on the island, about fifteen million strong, is made up of Chinese originating from the mainland Chinese province of Fujian. They followed the Hakka to Taiwan over the centuries. They speak the Taiwanese dialect of a Chinese language called Minnan (mee-NAHN).

Most of the remaining islanders are Waishengren (wie-SHEHN-grehn), or outsiders, whose families first arrived with Chiang Kai-Shek in 1949. Many of them spoke Standard Chinese or Mandarin, the northern version of the language. Standard Chinese is Taiwan's official language today.

Apart from the folk costumes of the minorities, dress for everyday use is much the same as elsewhere in the modern world—jeans, T-shirts, sweatshirts, suits, skirts, and shorts.

Religion

Taiwan has no official or state religion. Animism (a belief in spirits) lies behind many beliefs and rituals of both aboriginal and Chinese communities. Shamans, or *jitong* (jih-TAWNG)—men who go into a trance in order to communicate with the spirit world—still take part in many religious festivals. Over the ages such beliefs have become mingled with the three main faiths of China.

The first of these, Taoism, is based upon the teachings of Laozi (or Lao-Tzu), the "Old Master," who was honored after the 500s B.C.E. as the founder of the Taoist religion. He taught that life is governed by *Dao* (DOW), the harmonious relationship between the individual and the natural world. This religion later took on all sorts of beliefs in spirits, magical rituals, and in geomancy, by which buildings must be aligned in accordance with natural forces to achieve harmony and good fortune. Geomancy remains a planning priority today, even when modern skyscrapers are constructed.

The second main Chinese faith is Confucianism, based upon the ideas of Confucius (551–479 B.C.E.), or Kongfuzi. He emphasized harmony and peace within human society, rather than with nature. He believed in duty, truthfulness, and respect for one's rulers and one's parents. Confucian beliefs have shaped many social attitudes among Taiwan's Chinese, from politeness and hospitality to strangers to a respectful attitude toward those in authority.

Buddhism, the third faith, originated in India about 2,500 years ago. It is based on the teachings of Siddhartha Gautama, a prince who gave up all his worldly possessions in order to lead a simple life, eventually becoming the Buddha, or Enlightened One. Buddhists believe in karma and in the cycle of birth, life, death, and rebirth. The Buddha taught that human suffering is the result of desire and that release from desire can only be achieved through righteous behavior during many lives on Earth. In China, Buddhism grew to resemble a more conventional religion, with saints and bodhisattvas (boe-dee-SAHT-vahz: spirits), and the worship of a goddess of mercy called Avalokitesvara or Guanyin.

Taiwan is full of temples and shrines, many of them at least two hundred years old, ornate, and resplendent in gold and red. Some have figures of bodhisattvas, others of dragons and gods. There are said to be about eight thousand Taoist temples and about four thousand Buddhist temples on the island. However, it is sometimes hard to tell what religion is being observed, as over the ages they have become interwoven in a rich tapestry of beliefs.

The first Christian missionaries appeared in Taiwan about four hundred years ago. Today about 5 percent of the population are Protestant or Roman Catholic Christians.

Children sit by a colorful shrine dedicated to their ancestors. The honoring of ancestors plays an important part in the Confucian tradition.

Feeding the Ghosts

Chinese religious festivals take place on different days each year, since they follow the phases of the Moon rather than the Western calendar. The seventh month falls toward the end of the summer, in August or September. It is a somber time. According to the beliefs of many Taiwan Chinese, this is when ghosts and ancestral spirits return to walk the Earth. Offerings of food are left out for them, and paper money is burned for their use. Buddhist monks lead prayers to the spirits, and incense sticks are burned at shrines and temples. Many people fear that ghosts who have not been honored by their living relations will cause mischief to others. Not until the end of the seventh month do the shivers come to an end, as the spirits return to the underworld and life returns to normal.

All-Chinese Feasting

The everyday diet of Taiwan is a healthy one, including plenty of rice, fish, and fresh vegetables. Meals are eaten with chopsticks. Taiwanese food features noodles and dumplings, bean curd, and sauces flavored with soybeans, peppers, garlic, chilies, black beans, yellow beans, or plums. Local specialties include sweet potato, taro (an edible root), clams, and mussels.

Eating out is a regular habit for many, and there is a remarkable choice of restaurants. Immigrants from all over China have brought their own regional styles of cooking to the island. Restaurants serve Mongolian lamb hot pot, Szechuan pork with chili and peanuts, Peking duck, Hakka sausage, sweet-and-sour fish from Shanghai, and lemon chicken in Cantonese style.

Large amounts of tea are consumed every day, at home or at teahouses. It is drunk in the Chinese style, without milk. Alcoholic beverages include sweet rice wine and a strong liquor made from sorghum. Beer is served cold in bustling city bars, with bottles often decorated according to eye-catching themes. It is served with all sorts of tasty seafood snacks.

Going to Work

In mountainous Taiwan almost one-fourth of the land is suitable for growing crops, and more than one in ten workers farm the land. The most widespread crop is rice, grown in flooded paddies. Corn, soybeans, peanuts, taro, and sweet potatoes are other important food crops. Tea bushes are grown on the slopes of

Water buffalo are the mainstay of farming in eastern and southeastern Asia. This one is being used to haul a cart in K'en-ting, in southern Taiwan.

Nan-t'ou (nan-TOO) county in central Taiwan. Plantation workers, shaded from the hot sun with scarves and straw hats, pick the fresh green leaf tips and put them in the large baskets they carry on their backs. Taiwan's tropical climate is also perfect for sugarcane and for fruits such as bananas and pineapples. Cattle, hogs, goats, and poultry are raised on farms.

Taiwan's fishing fleet is large, supplying not just local consumers—for whom seafood forms a major part of their diet—but the fish markets of Japan, some of the busiest in the world.

Taiwan is not a large island, but it does have a number of useful resources, including coal, natural gas, limestone, and marble for quarrying. There are small amounts of copper, gold, and oil, but Taiwan has to import most of the fuel it needs for industry.

The Taiwanese economy was centrally planned under strict government control in the days of Chiang Kai-Shek. Today it is less regulated. Industrial workers make up a high proportion of the labor force (about 40 percent). Taiwanese factories produce textiles, footwear, cement, fertilizers, plastics, metal products, and bicycles. In the 1960s Taiwan was famed for its cheap toys and watches, the sort of products now manufactured in the People's Republic of China. In the 1990s Taiwan moved upmarket and now makes much of its money serving the international computer industry, producing personal computers, monitors, and silicon chips.

City Streets, Peaceful Gardens

The island has developed one of Asia's more successful "tiger" economies, and its high standard of living is reflected in the brash lifestyle of dwellers in cities such as the capital, Taipei, or the southwestern industrial port of Kao-hsiung (KAH-oe shih-YOONG), with its shopping malls, stores, hotels, karaoke bars, and nightclubs. The down side of modern development has been the industrial pollution of land, ocean, and air and the ravaging of beautiful countryside.

Taiwan's cities sprawl out across the plains, clogged with cabs and other traffic. The buildings are not ancient; indeed most of the concrete office and apartment buildings have been built

Taipei is a city of modern buildings intersected by long, straight streets and advertising billboards. High-rise development started taking place in the late 1970s.

during the last thirty years. However, public buildings, memorials, temples, and pavilions set in parks and gardens, or places of natural beauty, are often constructed according to the graceful models of traditional Chinese architecture.

Health and Education

Health care in Taiwan is largely private, covered by insurance plans. A female child can expect a life span of about seventy-nine years, a male of seventy-three years, figures that are better than in most of the People's Republic of China, but slightly lower than in Hong Kong.

Alongside Taiwan's modern hospitals are clinics dispensing traditional Chinese medicine, which makes use of herbal treatments, roots, leaves, and berries, as well as animal parts. Another ancient Chinese practice, now popular in many parts of the world, is acupuncture. Fine needles are inserted into the body in order to free up the flow of energy. The treatment is said to promote well-being and help some medical conditions, such as high blood pressure. Massage is popular, and many people seek treatments for ailments such as rheumatism and arthritis at mineral-rich hot springs, such as those beside the Chihpen (CHEE-pehn) River in the southeast of the island or at Lushan (loo-SHAHN) in the central mountains.

Education is a passion with many Taiwanese. All children must go to school between the ages of six and fifteen, and free schools are available. Science plays an important part in the curriculum, and vocational training between the ages of fifteen and eighteen has led to a workforce skilled in technology. About 95 percent of adult men and 93 percent of women can

Bathers relax in the healthy mineral waters of Chihpen hot springs, first developed during the Japanese occupation. There are hot and cool pools, fed by mountain streams.

read and write. A very high number of Taiwanese have a college education, and many study overseas, especially in the United States.

Craftworkers, Artists, and Performers

China has a long history of inventiveness, creativity, and design. Taiwan shares this tradition, which is expressed in pottery and porcelain, in carved jade, and in lacquerware. Lacquer is a kind of gum that is used as a decorative varnish for furniture and utensils.

Calligraphy, or fine writing, is valued as much as painting for artistic expression. The Chinese love of simplicity and harmony is expressed in paintings of nature. Taiwan has been more open than the People's Republic of China to the influence of international modern art, and this is reflected in some of the more experimental work to be seen in Taipei galleries.

Hakka Umbrellas

In a tropical climate with seasonal monsoon winds, an umbrella is essential as a protection against both sun and rain. Taiwanese factories make all sorts of modern umbrellas, but the ones that are admired as craft items are made by the Hakka people from a country town called Meinung (mae-NOONG), in Kaohsiung county. The umbrella frame is made of tough bamboo cane, harvested in the mountains. The covering is made of stiff paper, lacquered so that it is waterproof. The umbrellas are decorated by hand with paintings of blossoms, trees, birds, or women in costume. The umbrellas are not just suitable as souvenirs. They are tough and practical enough for everyday use. The craft of umbrella making was imported from the mainland about eighty years ago, and the Hakka umbrellas of Meinung soon became a favorite at home and abroad.

In music and theater, Chinese tradition thrives alongside more international influences. Chinese folk instruments may be heard in the parks, but Western rock and experimental music have also taken root in Taiwan, creating one of the liveliest popular music industries in the Far East.

Beijing opera is regularly acted out, with clashing cymbals and gongs. The stock characters from Chinese folklore are heavily made up to represent heroes or villains. These long productions are enlivened with dance, conjuring, and stunning acrobatics. Taiwanese actors have also developed their own, more informal versions of the opera, using local dialect and modern makeup.

Fighting Fit

The Chinese who sought refuge in Taiwan over the ages brought with them the martial arts of their homeland, such as kung fu. The aim of such exercises is not violence and aggression but the channeling of energy, well-being, and self-understanding. As on the Chinese mainland, the graceful, slow movements and controlled breathing of tai chi (TIE CHEE), a form of exercise characterized by a series of slow body movements, may be seen at first light in many parks and public places.

All sorts of sports are popular in Taiwan, from soccer to baseball, basketball, golf, and tennis. Swimming on the island's many beaches keeps young people fit, and there are many city swimming pools. More surprising in such a hot country, the mountain resort of Hohuan Shan (HOE-hwahn SHAHN), in the central mountains, receives enough snowfall for popular winter sports such as skiing.

The skiing season at the popular resort of Hohuan Shan, or "the mountain of harmonious happiness," lasts from January to March, when the snowfall is often heavy.

Firecrackers and Lanterns

Taiwan celebrates all the major festivals of the Chinese mainland. The Chinese New Year, or Spring Festival, is ushered in with deafening firecrackers, feasting, and the exchange of gifts. This is followed by the glowing beauty of the springtime Lantern Festival, the summer's exciting dragon boat races in Taipei, and the eating of sweet pastries, called moon cakes, to celebrate the full moon of autumn.

Taiwan also has many regional festivals, which celebrate local gods, shrines, temples, harvests and seasons, or commemorate famous events. One example is the summer festival in honor of Cheng Huang, the god believed to protect the city of Taipei. It is marked by processions, feasting, and dancing.

Taiwan's nonreligious festivals, such as Republic Day (January 1) and Taiwan Restoration Day (October 25), are also marked with dancing, music, and parades.

A mother and her two small children carry lanterns during a Chinese New Year celebration at the Chiang Kai-Shek Memorial in Taiwan's capital city, Taipei.

In Honor of Ma-tsu Tao

Ma-tsu Tao is revered around the South China Sea as the protector of seafarers and is honored with a special cult on the island of Taiwan, where she has become a patron saint. Ma-tsu Tao may have been a historical figure called Lin Mo-liang, who lived from 960 to 1127 C.E. She is said to have performed various miracles, saving lives at sea. Ma-tsu Tao led such a pure life that she came to be remembered as a saint or goddess and has some five hundred shrines and temples dedicated to her in Taiwan. In March each year

Ma-tsu Tao's image is carried through central Taiwan in a spectacular procession, with beating drums, chanting, clouds of incense, exploding firecrackers, paper money being burned as an offering, and acrobatics and martial arts exhibitions. Tens of thousands of Taiwanese take part, in the hope of receiving the blessing of Ma-tsu Tao. The procession takes eight days and visits fifty-nine different temples over a distance of 175 miles (280 kilometers). Processions and festivals take place at many other sites as well.

THAILAND

THAILAND FORMS A BRIDGE BETWEEN THE INDIAN AND PACIFIC OCEANS.
It occupies the Southeast Asian mainland between Myanmar in the west
and Laos and Cambodia in the east. A long, narrow strip of territory
stretches south to form a border with Malaysia.

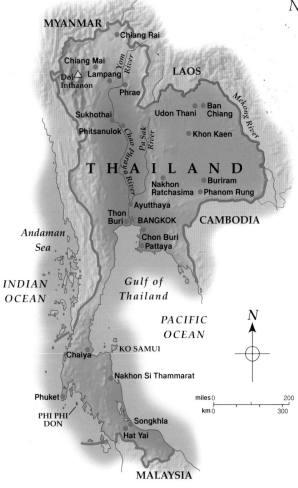

*Northern Thailand is a highland region, reaching
8,512 feet (2,594 meters) above sea level at Doi
Inthanon. From there, mountain streams descend
to the Chao Phraya River. This rolls across the
fertile central plain, finally flowing into the
Gulf of Thailand. Eastern Thailand forms a
basin that drains into the Mekong River, on
the border with Laos. The southern
panhandle is a land of tropical rain forests
fringed by beaches and palms.*

Three grinning Shan boys climb into a specially
decorated cab, or tuk-tuk. They are celebrating the Poy
Sang Long Festival, in which boys are initiated as
Buddhist monks.

The Golden Land

Thailand (TIE-land) lies on the chief land and sea routes between the Indian subcontinent and Southeast Asia. Bands of hunters were roaming through its forests at least forty thousand years ago, and by twelve thousand years ago its inhabitants had learned how to cultivate rice, a crop that has been harvested at the end of the rainy season every year since.

The early technology of Thailand (previously called Siam) was remarkable—pottery remains date back as early as 6800 B.C.E. Traces of bronze working discovered at Ban Chiang (BAHN chee-ANG), in the northeast of the country, may be four thousand years old. This suggests

These decorated pots were discovered at the Bronze Age settlement of Ban Chiang, to the east of Udon Thani. They are about six thousand years old.

FACTS AND FIGURES

Official name: Kingdom of Thailand

Status: Independent state

Capital: Bangkok

Major towns: Chiang Mai, Hat Yai, Kohn Kaen, Buriram, Songkhla, Chon Buri, Nakhon Si Thammarat, Phitsanulok, Nakhon Ratchasima

Area: 198,455 square miles (513,998 square kilometers)

Population: 63,100,000

Population density: 318 per square mile (123 per square kilometer)

Peoples: 75 percent Thai; 14 percent Chinese; 5 percent Malays; 6 percent others, including Akha, Hmong, Karen, Mon, Nyaw, Shan, and Yao

Official language: Thai

Currency: Baht

National days: Birthday of King Bhumibol Adulyadej (December 5); Constitution Day (December 10)

Country's name: Thailand means "Land of the Thai people."

that the region was among the earliest in the world to produce this precious alloy and was home to the most advanced civilization in Southeast Asia at that time.

In about 200 B.C.E. Buddhist monks arrived from India (see INDIA), bringing their faith to what they called "the Golden Land." The most widespread inhabitants of the country at that time were the Mon (MAWN), a Southeast Asian people who

Time line:	Rice is being cultivated in Thailand	Evidence of the first pottery	Indian monks bring Buddhism to Thailand
	ca. 10,000 B.C.E.	ca. 6800 B.C.E.	ca. 200 B.C.E.

CLIMATE

Thailand has a tropical climate. From March to May the weather is very hot. Monsoon winds start bringing rainfall in May, becoming torrential in September and October. A cooler season lasts through to spring. At high altitudes in the north it can be quite cold, and the far southwest gets the heaviest rains.

	Bangkok	Chiang Mai	Phuket
Average January temperature:	*78°F* *(26°C)*	*70°F* *(21°C)*	*81°F* *(27°C)*
Average July temperature:	*83°F* *(28°C)*	*81°F* *(27°C)*	*83°F* *(28°C)*
Average annual precipitation:	*56 in.* *(142 cm)*	*47 in.* *(119 cm)*	*92 in.* *(234 cm)*

also played an important part in the early history of Myanmar (see MYANMAR). The Mon Buddhist states that developed from this period onward, centered upon the Chao Phraya (CHAH-oe PRIE-yuh) basin, were known collectively as Dvaravati (duh-vah-ruh-VAH-tee). Between the 500s and 800s C.E. they prospered and traded with India.

Indian ties also played a strong part in the development of a southern state called Lankasuka (lang-kuh-SOO-kuh), based on what is now the town of Nakhon Si Thammarat (NAH-kawn SEE TAM-muh-raht). It extended down the Malay Peninsula. By the 700s this was governed by the Buddhist Srivijaya (sree-wih-JAW-yuh) empire, a powerful seafaring state based on the island of Sumatra (now in Indonesia: see INDONESIA). Srivijaya rule extended north to

The Khmer temple complex at Phanom Rung is the finest example of Khmer architecture in Thailand. More than a thousand years old, the temple seen here was restored from 1971 to 1988.

Mon kingdoms prosper within the Dvaravati federation	Southern kingdom of Lankasuka becomes part of Srivijaya empire	Khmer rule much of Thailand
500–800 C.E.	**700s**	**800s–900s**

Chaiya (CHIE-uh). Its legacy includes the remains of temples and fine statues.

In the 800s and 900s both Dvaravati and Srivijaya were threatened by the Khmer (kuh-MUHR) people of Cambodia (see CAMBODIA). As the Khmer states were unified, their rulers became more powerful and pushed into neighboring regions, becoming overlords of Thailand. Their wealth grew through trade, and they spent fortunes on the building of temples.

Kingdoms of the Thai

The original homeland of the Thai people was in Sichuan (SEHCH-wahn), in China (see CHINA). In the 600s they migrated southward and founded a kingdom called Nanchao (nan-CHAH-oe) on China's southern borders. Soon the Thai were pushed farther southward into Thailand and Myanmar, fleeing the growing power of the Chinese empire. Migration into Thailand continued for about five centuries, until they outnumbered the Mon.

During the 1200s Khmer power declined to the east. To the north, Mongol (MAWN-goel) armies from the steppe grasslands of central Asia invaded China. Mongol-Chinese armies then moved onward into Nanchao and Southeast Asia. The Thai decided it was time to unite in self-defense and to determine their own future.

In 1238 two Thai princes broke away from Khmer dominion and created an independent kingdom, based in Sukhothai (SOO-koe-tie), a city on the central plains, beside the Yom (YAWM) River. This remained the capital until 1376. The city

White Elephants

Buddhist scriptures tell of a "white elephant," and such animals really do exist. They are albino elephants, pale-skinned if not actually white, and have been held sacred by the kings of Thailand ever since the days of Ramkhamhaeng. Every elephant owned by a king must prove that it is docile and well trained. The phrase white elephant *has passed into general use, meaning an expensive folly, a project that turns out to be a waste of time. That is said to be because the Thai kings would sometimes give a white elephant as a gift to a courtier or another king. The recipient had to spend a fortune looking after the sacred beast and feeding it, but could never put it to profitable work lest he offend the king and the priests. Anxiety at the expense of maintenance soon outweighed any gratitude at having been honored by the king in this way.*

grew over the years, to include wooden palaces, fine houses, shining lakes, and temples of stone. Beyond the city walls, a further forty temples spread across the plains, as witness to the piety of its Buddhist rulers. From small beginnings, Sukhothai power spread rapidly. Ramkhamhaeng, who came to the throne in 1278, extended his power over large areas of Thailand and also controlled parts of Myanmar and Laos (see LAOS).

The founding of the Sukhothai kingdom	The rise of the Lanna kingdom	Ayutthaya state is founded	Portuguese, Dutch, and British trade with Ayutthaya
1238	**1259–1281**	**1351**	**1500s**

Other independent kingdoms, or city-states, thrived alongside that of Sukhothai. The most important of these was a northern Thai kingdom called Lanna (LAH-nuh), which was carved out from Mon territory between 1259 and 1281 by a ruler called Mengrai. A new Lanna capital was founded at Chiang Mai (chee-YANG MIE) in 1292, and this, too, became a great center of culture and temple building. Sukhothai power declined in the 1320s, but Lanna would thrive for another two hundred years or so.

However, a new Thai city was now on the rise. Ayutthaya (ah-yoo-TIE-uh)—or Phra Nakhon Si Ayutthaya in full—was founded in 1351 by a prince called U Thong, who as king took the name of Ramathibodi I. His state prospered and grew. In 1432 King Boromraja II invaded Cambodia and captured its capital, Angkor. By 1438 Ayutthaya had absorbed the kingdom of Sukhothai, and in the 1500s it came to occupy much the same areas as Thailand does today. By the late 1600s Ayutthaya was already home to about a million people. Many of them were boat dwellers—the city was sited on an island at the meeting point of the Chao Phraya and Pa Sak (PAH SAHK) Rivers. The city traded with India, China, and by the 1500s, increasingly with Europeans, such as the Portuguese, the Dutch, and the British. Ayutthaya soon controlled much of Thailand.

This period of prosperity and expansion was marred only by wars with the Burmans of Myanmar. The first of these was a brutal and bloody conflict resulting in the fall of Ayutthaya in 1569. A Thai army won the city back twenty years later, and the Thai economy and culture prospered once again. However, in the 1760s the Burman armies returned, and in 1767 Ayutthaya was destroyed and its people killed or led away to captivity.

Free Thailand

War with China soon forced the Burmans to withdraw from Thailand. The Thai people then moved their capital downstream to Thon Buri (TAWN-boo-ree). Under the reign of Rama I (1782–1809), the seat of power was moved across the Chao Phraya River to Bangkok (BANG-kawk). The new city was an immediate success and enjoyed stable rule under the Chakri (SHAHK-ree) dynasty.

As European colonialists prowled around Southeast Asia, looking for new colonies to exploit, the kings of Thailand played a clever diplomatic game. They allowed the Westerners concessions, but made sure that no single foreign power was favored. During the reigns of Mongkut (1851–1868) and his son Rama V (1868–1910), wealth from trade was used to modernize the country. The royal family made a point of learning about Western culture in order to understand the new balance of power in Asia. As a result, Thailand became the only country in Southeast Asia to escape European colonial rule, although in the years that followed it did lose a great deal of territory to France and Britain. The worst losses occured after 1893 when the French bullied Thailand out of possession of its

The fall of Ayutthaya	Ayutthaya destroyed by Burmans from Myanmar	New kingdom established at Thon Buri	Rama I establishes Bangkok as capital of all Siam
1569	**1767**	**1767–1782**	**1782–1809**

A wealthy Thai lady poses for the photographer with her servants in about 1900. Note her elaborate, traditional costume, headdress, and jewelry.

coup in 1932, during worldwide economic problems known as the Great Depression, led to real power being removed from Rama VII (reigned 1925–1935). In 1935 he handed over royal power to Prince Ananda Mahidol. The centuries of Thai kings holding absolute, personal power had come to an end. The monarchy was now constitutional, governed by the laws of the country.

An Era of Change

There followed a power struggle between the socialists, who wished to bring the economy under central-state control, and the extremely conservative military. During World War II (1939–1945), the government of Thailand supported Japan. As Japanese armies invaded Southeast Asia and defeated the European colonial powers, the Thai government hoped to regain territory it had lost to France in Cambodia. It also wished to expand its borders, bringing Thai communities in neighboring countries under its rule. However, many Thais opposed the Japanese, and a resistance movement was founded with American support. Japan was defeated in 1945.

After the war, King Ananda was assassinated. His replacement was King Bhumibol (Rama IX). He has been a stabilizing influence during an almost continuous struggle for power between the

Cambodian and Laotian territories, which were eventually united with Vietnam as part of French Indochina.

In the twentieth century the kings of Thailand had to face even more severe crises. Rama VI, who reigned from 1910 to 1925, saw his country through World War I (1914–1918) and from 1917 backed the winning side. This insurance policy helped Thailand keep its independence in the years that followed. However, a bloodless

Modernization under Mongkut	Further modernization and reform under Rama V	Coup followed by constitutional monarchy	Siam is renamed Thailand and supports Japan in World War II
1851–1868	**1868–1910**	**1932–1935**	**1939–1945**

Planning the future. Thai Prime Minister Thaksin Shinawatra (center) appears with veteran ruler King Bhumibol (right) in 2003.

military and more democratic politicians. The last fifty years have been marked by coups, repression of civil liberties, corrupt elections, and periods of social unrest.

Southeast Asia was in crisis during the Cold War (1945–1990), a period of worldwide tension between the U.S.S.R. and other communist countries on one side and the United States and its Western allies on the other. Thailand sided with the West, and the United States poured in financial support. This reached a peak in the sixties and seventies, during the Vietnam War. Thailand grew industrially, attracted foreign investment, and developed one of the most successful tourist industries in the world, but many of the poor remained poor and the Western influx caused dislocation of traditional Thai values.

Despite economic improvements, many Thais felt growing anger at political corruption, such as the buying of votes at elections. They called for proper democracy and accountability. Protests peaked in 1992, but were brutally suppressed, to the expressed anger of King Bhumibol. Elections were held in 1995, and a new constitution was signed by the king in 1997.

Thailand's Government

Thailand was becoming more democratic, although critics complained that big business was now just as powerful in government as the military had been before. The fairness of the 2001 election was disputed, too. It brought to power as Prime Minister Thaksin Shinawatra, head of a new political party called Thai Rak Thai.

Other political parties include the Democratic Party (DP), the National Development Party (NDP), and the Thai National Party (TNP). The National Assembly has two Houses, a Senate or *Wuthisapha*, and the House of Representatives or *Sapha Phuthaen Ratsadon*.

Cold War; Thailand becomes key regional ally of the United States	King Bhumibol (Rama IX) signs new constitution	Thaksin Shinawatra wins election
1945–1990	**1997**	**2001**

Peoples of Plains and Coasts

The Thai people's traditions and customs developed out of a peasant culture. They were shaped over the ages by village life and the timeless cycle of planting and harvesting rice. Other major social influences were the rituals of the Buddhist faith and the royal court, and a social system known as *sakdina* (sahk-DEE-nuh), whereby peasants would be recruited to carry out public works or military service.

The Thai have been merchants over many centuries, and today many are successful businesspeople. Making up about 75 percent of the national population, the Thai live in all parts of the country, but they are concentrated on the plains and in the cities. They are the largest part of a broad ethnic group that also takes in the Dai of the Yunnan province of southwestern China, the Thai of Vietnam, the Lao of Laos, and the Shan of Myanmar. There are also overseas communities of Thai, many having settled in Western countries and Australia. All speak related languages, although experts argue as to just how these fit into the linguistic patterns and groupings of eastern Asia.

International dress is largely worn on the streets of modern Thailand—dresses, shirts, pants, jeans, T-shirts, shorts, and sandals. Cool cotton is favored in this tropical climate. Traditional Thai costume is also seen, especially in the countryside. Men wear a sarong (suh-RAWNG), or cloth, wrapped around the waist, below a loose shirt without a collar. Women wear a sarong with a blouse. On formal occasions, they may glitter with jewels and silk.

The beautiful Thai script dates back to the Sukhothai period. It is said to have been devised by King Ramkhamhaeng in 1283, although it may well be older in origin. The script is an alphabet made up

---

Let's Talk Thai

The Thai language is spoken throughout Thailand, but its dialects vary greatly between north and south, and the Lao version of the language is spoken in the northeast. The standard, official form of the language is based upon the Krung Thep, or Bangkok, dialect. Many non-Thai minorities also speak Thai as a first or second language. Thai is a language that, like Chinese, relies on slight variations in tone to convey very different meanings. There are five possible tones indicated by accent — low, high, middle, rising, and falling.

Sawàt dii (suh-WAHT DEE)	*Hello/Goodbye*
Khàwp khun (KAWP KOON)	*Thank you*
nèung, sâwng, sâam, sii, hâa (NEH-yoong, SAWNG, suh-AHM, SEE, huh-AH)	*one, two, three, four, five*
khwāa, sái (KWAA, SIE)	*right, left*
Kii mohng láew? (kih MAWNG lah-YOO)	*What's the time?*
ahān (uh-HAHNG)	*food*
khâo (KHAH-oe)	*rice*
kway tiaw (KWAE tee-YAW)	*noodles*
chaa	*tea*

---

of forty-four consonants, eighteen vowels, and six diphthongs (combined letters).

About 14 percent of the Thai population is ethnically Chinese, and one-third of these live in the capital, Bangkok. They speak a number of different Chinese languages, including Standard Chinese, or Mandarin. Languages of southern China, such as Yue (yoo-WAE), also known as Cantonese; Hakka (HAH-kuh); and Mindong (mihn-DAWNG) and Minnan (mee-NAHN), both from the Min dialectal family, are more commonly spoken. They are well integrated into Thai society.

The Mon people, who played such a strong role in the early civilization of Thailand, are today outnumbered by later arrivals. Their chief areas of settlement are in the west of the country and to the north of Bangkok; many are rice farmers. Three million Mon live in Thailand today. Their numbers have increased greatly over the past several centuries due to Mon refugees from across the Myanmar border, fleeing persecution. The Mon way of life and religious beliefs are much the same as those of the Thai, and they have become closely integrated into Thai society, many learning the Thai language.

A woman of the Yao minority in the northern province of Chiang Rai. She wears the traditional turban and collar and holds a basket on her back.

The headdresses of these Akha women contrast with the informal, modern clothes of the youngsters. Most Akha live in Chiang Mai, Chiang Rai, Lampang, and Phrae.

Hill Peoples

Seventy-five different languages have been recorded in Thailand, but many of these are only spoken by very small, scattered communities. The highland regions of the north are home to a rich mixture of peoples and cultures, increased in the last thirty years by refugees escaping conflict or oppression in neighboring lands.

The largest of the mountain minorities is that of the Karen (kuh-REHN), or Kariang (kuh-ree-ANG). Their chief homeland is across the Myanmar border, but half a million or so live within Thailand. They cultivate rice paddies and live in villages of stilt houses. The men are expert elephant handlers, although the use of these animals for logging has declined in Thailand. Karen women are famous weavers. They produce beautiful sarongs, often in red with stripes of other colors, on back-strap looms (in which the threads are tied to a beam and tensioned by a belt worn around the waist).

The Hmong (huh-MAWNG), also known as Miao (mee-YAH-oe) or Meo, number over sixty thousand in Thailand. They, too, are a farming people, part of a larger regional ethnic group whose range also takes in parts of southern China, Laos, Myanmar, and Vietnam. They are world famous for their blue and black costumes, which are embroidered with intricate designs in pink and red and worn with heavy silver jewelry.

The related Yao (YAH-oe) are scattered over a similar portion of Southeast Asia. In Thailand they have a population of approximately forty thousand. They have their own written language, and the traditional costume of their women also dazzles the eye, with embroidered pants and jackets of black or indigo, set off by red collars.

Long ago, the Akha (AHK-huh), known to the Thais as Kaw (KAW), inhabited the far northwest Tibetan plateau. After centuries of migration through China, they reached Myanmar and Thailand, less than one hundred years ago. More recently, Akha have been fleeing into Thailand because of oppression in Myanmar, and today they number about sixty thousand. The women wear elaborate, plumed headdresses made of beads or coins.

Thailand's thirty thousand Lisu (LEE-soo), or Lisaw, have a similar history to the Akha. Their traditional costume is also spectacularly colorful. Another ethnic group of Tibetan origin is the Lahu (LAH-hoo), of whom about twenty-eight thousand live near the Myanmar border.

In the hills of Chiang Rai province a typical village dwelling, such as the one seen here, has a thatched roof and is supported by tall wooden stilts.

Customs in the Hills

Thailand's Chao Khao (CHAH-oe KAH-oe), or hill peoples, are facing great changes, brought about by development in communications and transportation, tourism, farming methods and land use, education, and modern medicine. The traditional way of life does survive in many ways, however.

- *At a Mien (mee-EHN) wedding, the bride's hair is covered in beeswax and pushed into a towering structure of sticks, cloth, tassels, and fringes.*

- *The Lahu play pipes made of five lengths of bamboo cane, each fitted with a reed, stuck into a gourd as a sounding box. When a young man and woman are dating, they play tunes to each other on this musical instrument, which is called a* naw *(NAW).*

- *An old Lisu belief is that people can become possessed by vampires. These are said to take the form of an animal and suck blood from living people or corpses to stay alive. Vampires may be scared away from graves by the sound of gunshots.*

- *The Akha build "spirit gates" at the entrances to each village, guarded by wooden statues of a man and woman. The gate is believed to protect the village from the spirits of the forest.*

- *To decide where to build a new settlement, an Akha village elder will clear a patch of ground and then drop an egg on to the soil. If it breaks, then the spirits are believed to have allowed the building to commence. If it does not, then they move elsewhere.*

The Lawa (LAH-wah), or Lua (LOO-ah), are another rice-growing northern people, about fourteen thousand strong. Related to the Mon, they probably originated in Cambodia but were in Thailand before the Thais themselves.

Spirit Houses and Wats

Ninety-five percent of the population in Thailand is Buddhist, so one might expect that religious beliefs are fairly uniform. However, the opposite is true—Thai culture brings together many different strands of faith. The oldest beliefs of eastern Asia are still found among some of the hill peoples. These include a belief in spirits and awe for the shamans, community leaders who fall into a trance in order to speak directly to the spirit world. Offerings of food are made to the spirits. Honoring one's ancestors is another important aspect of these ancient beliefs. Some hill peoples have adopted Christianity or Buddhism.

Many mainstream Thai Buddhists believe in spirits. Model "spirit houses" are erected outside many houses to provide a home for spirits and to prevent them from entering the real house. Buddhists are usually superstitious, and many wear charms or a small image of the Buddha for good luck.

Buddhism has been the leading force in Thai life for about eighteen hundred years. The religion came from India and is based upon the teachings of Siddhartha Gautama (ca. 563–483 B.C.E.), who came to be known as the Buddha or Enlightened One. The branch of Buddhism that took root in

These spirit houses, on the beautiful southern island of Ko Samui, are built to protect a village from the influence of malign spirits.

Many temples in Thailand also honor Hindu gods, especially Vishnu, Preserver of the World. Buddhism and Hinduism share common roots, and Thailand's ancient links with India have encouraged this close association. Many Thai kings have assumed the name of Rama, honored in Hindu mythology as an incarnation or form of Vishnu. The historic Thai city of Ayutthaya was named after Ajodhya in India, where Rama was a prince.

Thailand is called Theravada. It emphasizes the importance of following the simple life of a monk, and as a symbol of this, every Thai male is expected to become a monk for a brief period of his life. Many men become full-time Buddhist monks, spending each day in meditation, chanting, or collecting alms (money or assistance given as charity to the poor). Monks are present at weddings and funerals, and often bless the construction of a new home.

Buddhist temples, or wats (WAHTZ), are often elaborate, beautiful buildings. They may serve as monasteries, as places of pilgrimage, as the center of religious festivals, and as meeting places for the community. The most sacred temple of all is Wat Phra Kaeo, an ornate, gilded complex decorated with demons, snakes, and gods. It stands within the Royal Palace in Bangkok, which was built in 1785, and is home to a small, but much revered, jade statue known as the Emerald Buddha.

Dragons writhe around a stairway at the Wat Bupparam, a temple in Chiang Mai that houses a four-hundred-year-old Buddha carved from black teak.

About 4 percent of Thais are Muslims. They are mostly located in the south of the country. Muslims believe in a single God, Allah, whose messenger on Earth was the prophet Muhammad, who lived in Arabia from about 570 to 632. Muslims must pray five times daily and worship each Friday in the local mosque.

Prawns and Lemongrass

Rice is the chief crop and the staple food, eaten at almost every meal. Noodles also form the basis of many dishes, especially at lunchtime. Most meals are served in the home, but there are also many restaurants serving Thai food. Tanks containing live fish or crustaceans for selection by the customer are common. Most food is eaten with fork and spoon, but chopsticks may be used to eat noodles, and in the north the right hand may be used to eat the sticky form of rice popular there.

In the cool of the tropical evening, many Thais head for the nearest "night market." Here, amid the bustle of the city, street vendors set up stalls under the lights and dish out sizzling snacks, rice, noodles, pancakes, chicken, fish, soups, stews, desserts, and fruit beverages.

Immigrants from Thailand have made their national dishes famous around the world. Thai food combines elements of Indian, Chinese, and Malay cooking. Very hot curries, sweet and sour sauces, soups, and stir-fry are common dishes. Popular ingredients include chicken, eggs, pork in the north, and seafood such as prawns and squid in the south. The heat of chili peppers is balanced by more subtle flavors and fragrances afforded by garlic, mint, coriander, lemongrass, pandanus leaves (a tropical plant resembling a palm), ginger, fish sauce, and coconut. Tropical fruits, including mangoes, pineapples, bananas, and papayas, are served in salads and desserts. Fruits and vegetables are often carved into floral designs for the dinner table. Beverages include tea or coffee, fruit juices, coconut milk, sugarcane juice, and beer.

Thai Stir-Fried Vegetables

This vegetable dish is popular in Thailand, as a side order as well as a main dish. Use vegetables you like, and simply vary amounts depending on how many people you are serving. Below is a list of some vegetables that you might like to try out.

2 tbsp (30 grams) peanut oil
1 tbsp (15 grams) light soy sauce
spinach leaves, sliced
broccoli florets
carrots, sliced
cauliflower florets
peppers, mixed red and green
snow peas
mushrooms, sliced
shallots (small red or purple onions), sliced
2 tbsp (30 grams) lime juice
1 tbsp (15 grams) sugar
bean sprouts

Heat a little peanut oil in a wok or skillet over medium heat and stir in the soy sauce. Add all the other ingredients except the sugar and bean sprouts.

Stir fry until just cooked (the vegetables should still be crispy). Add sugar to taste. If the mixture becomes too dry, add a little water. Remove from the heat, stir in the bean sprouts, and serve with rice.

Life on the Land

Country villages may form a nucleus surrounded by flooded fields called paddies, or else be strung out along roads, canals, riverbanks, or coastlines. Houses are traditionally of bamboo or teak timbers and are often built on stilts to avoid monsoon flooding or infestation by snakes.

Thailand's poor farmers work hard in the fields, with little modern machinery to help them. Farm animals in Thailand include water buffalo, oxen, and hogs. Chickens are raised in large numbers, and ducks are valued for both eggs and meat. A widespread switch to the growing of cash crops, in areas where people formerly farmed just for local consumption, has caused upheaval in rural society, as small farms are taken over by wealthy landowners or companies.

Heavy rainfall and fertile river basins make the land in Thailand ideal for growing rice. Drier areas rely on irrigation. Half of all farmland is used to grow rice, grown in paddies or by dry cultivation in the hills. Forty percent of the rice crop is exported, making Thailand one of the world's leading producers.

Grain crops, important in feeding livestock, include corn and sorghum. Other food crops include lush tropical fruits, sugarcane, soybeans, peanuts, sesame, tapioca, and coconut. Fiber crops are grown too, such as cotton, jute (a coarse fiber used for sacking), and kapok (a fluffy fiber from tree seeds, used for insulation and padding).

Thanks to the monsoon rains, Thailand has large areas of tropical rain forest with precious hardwoods such as teak. However, between 1960 and 1990 the country's total forested area was almost halved, the result of commercial logging (often illegal); clearance for firewood; and agricultural, industrial, and urban development. Since the 1990s, plans for conservation, forest management, logging bans, and the planting of new trees have been implemented. It is not just a question of saving resources, but a matter of conserving the landscape. Tree roots trap precious moisture in the soil and prevent erosion.

Fishing

Thailand is a major fishing nation. Frozen or dried shrimps, prawns, and squid, as well as canned tuna, are exported as far away as the United States and Europe.

Irrigation does not necessarily need expensive technology. A boy sprinkles water from a can over a field during a dry spell on the island of Ko Samui.

The village of Bo Sang, in Chiang Mai, is famous for its painted umbrellas and parasols, which are made by hand from mulberry paper, cotton, or silk.

Freshwater fish for the home market are caught in lakes and rivers, often by large scoop nets, which are lowered into the water on long poles. Southeast Asian fishing zones have been a source of dispute between Thailand and its neighbors in recent years.

Resources and Industries

Thailand has natural gas fields offshore in the Gulf of Thailand, but not much oil. Lignite, a low-grade form of coal, is an alternative fuel. Metal ores include tin, copper, and gold. The country also mines precious rubies and sapphires. Industrial pollution of the environment is widespread. For example, the large amounts of water used in tin mining may wash poisons into the soil.

Thai factories produce cotton textiles and garments, footwear, processed foods, wooden furniture, vehicles, electronic goods and computers, cement, and plastics. Finance and other service industries are growing fast, their workers accounting for 49 percent of the labor force, as opposed to 40 percent in industry and just 11 percent in agriculture. Millions of foreign tourists are attracted to Thailand's beaches, cities, and hills, bringing in much needed wealth and providing a market for local handicrafts and produce.

Southeast Asia is a poor part of the world, but Thailand does have a better standard of living than its neighbors, with the exception of Singapore and Malaysia.

City Streets

Thirty-one percent of Thailand's population lives in towns or cities. All of these are dwarfed by the capital, Bangkok, which is now a teeming city of some nine million people. Cities are

As evening falls in Bangkok, bright lights are switched on for the night market. All kinds of delicious Thai snacks and foodstuffs are laid out in the stalls.

Bangkok

Bangkok was originally a small settlement on the bank of the Chao Phraya River. In 1782 King Rama I decided to move the capital there from Thon Buri. He wanted to give his new city an impressive name, which, rather like an advertising slogan of its day, listed all its marvels, including its gems, its royal palaces, its temples, and its powerful spirits. These all added up to what is said to have been the longest place name ever recorded:

Krungthep Mahanakhon Bovorn Ratanakosin Mahintha Rayutthaya Mahadilokpop Noparatrachathani Burirom Udomratchanivetmahasathan Amornpiman Avatarnsathit Sakkathattiyavisnukarmprasit.
As this was such a mouthful to say, the Thai simply called it Krung Thep (KROONG THEHP), and still do today — although most of them can recite the name in full!

swelling with country people coming in search of their fortune. Bangkok is at the center of everything, a hub of national communications, industry, commerce, tourism, and transportation by road, air, rail, or boat.

The low-lying capital city of Thailand sprawls out across the plain from the banks of the Chao Phraya River and a network of canals. Bangkok has a grand royal palace, glittering temples, galleries, embassies, and hotels. The city is a center of entertainment and culture. It has floating markets, where fruit and vegetables are sold from small wooden boats. Bangkok also has vast areas of modern stores and apartment

The inner-city speed limit in Bangkok is fairly high, but congested roads make city travel slow. Traffic drives on the left-hand side of the road. Public transportation is cheap and efficient.

Tuk-tuks *and Long-tails*

One job a country boy may find in a city is that of cab driver. Thailand has many cabs — and only a few of them are cars. The samlor *(SAM-LOER) is a bicycle attached to a rickshaw. This three-wheeler is generally pedal-powered and requires a* lot of muscle power to get it going. *Another three-wheeler, the motor-powered rickshaw, is known endearingly as a tuk-tuk (TOOK-TOOK), because of the noise made by its lawnmower-like engine. Tuk-tuks are designed to carry three passengers in their cab, but they often cram in more as they hurtle around the streets. In many towns* songthaews *(sawng-TAH-oez: larger vehicles with benches in the back) can be hailed. These are often shared among several passengers and follow set routes. Finally, Thailand's canals and rivers are plied by water-taxis, long-tail boats with powerful engines. These can carry up to twenty passengers.*

A long-tail boat, moored on the north coast of Phi Phi Don Island, casts its long, narrow shadow. Water transportation plays an important role in Thailand.

buildings, crowded streets, traffic jams, noise, and pollution. Some districts are full of seedy clubs and bars.

Social Facts and Figures

Thai cities have modern hospitals and clinics, and poorer families are entitled to free health care. However, in the countryside and mountains, provision is more basic, with about twenty-five doctors per 100,000 people. Many people rely on monks or on traditional healers who use folk medicines based on herbs and animal extracts. Life expectancy in the nation as a whole is sixty-eight years for men and seventy-five years for women. Common illnesses include malaria and dengue fever, which are spread by mosquito bites, heart disease, and HIV/AIDS.

Education was a long-standing responsibility of Buddhist monks, but today most schools are private or public (free) state-run schools. In the 1990s the number of years for which children had to attend school was raised from six to nine. Most children receive elementary level education, but few proceed to higher levels. Thailand has colleges in most major cities.

Ninety-six percent of adult males and 90 percent of adult females are able to read and write. There is a great variety of Thai-language newspapers and magazines on sale in the towns, including the mass-circulation *Thai Rath* and the more serious *Siam Rath*. The English-language press includes *The Nation* and the *Bangkok Post*.

There is no strict censorship, but, nevertheless, the powerful influence of government, business, and the military extends across the communications media. The main terrestrial television station is Channel 9, and there are four other channels available in parts of the country, as well as cable and satellite services.

Sporting Thais

Thais have a lively interest in international sports such as soccer, tennis, and basketball, and regional sports also have a huge following. *Takraw* (TAHK-rahw), for example, is played using a light ball of rattan cane or plastic, which must be kept in the air using any part of the body except the hands. *Muay* (moo-WAE) Thai or Thai boxing is also popular. Any part of the body may be used to attack one's opponent; leaping and kicking form part of the action. It is much more than a conventional boxing method. It is more of a martial art that claims to promote self-awareness and concentration. Thai boxing has high entertainment value, too, often being performed to a musical accompaniment and to large crowds, as well as being shown on national television.

A class troops down the steps of a Bangkok school at the end of a busy day. The pupils carry their bags of workbooks and homework.

559

A female drummer joins a traditional Thai orchestra during a show for tourists at the crowded east-coast resort of Pattaya.

Art, Dance, and Music

The Thai people have a rich cultural history, stretching back to the first medieval kingdoms. It is expressed in the craftwork of villagers, in basketry, weaving, silk, jewelry, and metalwork. It finds artistic expression in the form of statues (often graceful and moving images of the Buddha), in splendid and ornate temple architecture, and in poetry.

An enduring inspiration has been the ancient Indian tale of good and evil, the *Ramayana*, which became known in Thailand during the Khmer period and inspired a Thai version, the *Ramakien* (ruh-MAH-kee-ehn). The epic tale is retold in wall paintings, dance, theater, music, and even puppetry.

Traditional Thai dance-dramas take on various forms, originally dictated by the social status of the audience. *Khon* (KAWN) is a form of dance that tells a story, once performed only for the royal court. The dancers act out the roles of humans, gods, masked monkeys, and demons. In recent years these performances have been revived with modern audio-visual technology and special effects. *Lakhon* (LAH-kawn) is another dance form, often retelling traditional folktales with an all-female, unmasked cast.

Thai dance is much admired for its graceful and sinuous movements and is most commonly performed by an ensemble of eight to twelve dancers. Its dazzling costumes and headdresses vary from one region of Thailand to another. Standard performances include dances with scarves, candles, brass "fingernails" 6 inches (15 cm) long, and anklets, all of which serve to accentuate the stylized hand and foot gestures.

Likay (lih-KAE) is a popular form of folk drama, a kind of outrageous pantomime using comedy and satire. It is performed at fairs and festivals around the country. Puppetry is another popular Thai tradition. Shadow puppets, as used in Malaysia and Indonesia, are flat figures made of leather that are manipulated behind an illuminated screen. Costumed marionettes, made of paper and wire, are also popular.

Orchestras make use of drums, gongs, xylophones, oboes, flutes, and fiddles. Traditional Thai music originally developed at the royal court as an accompaniment to dance, as well as from temple chants and festivals, and as an accompaniment to rural folk dance.

Not all Thai culture derives from tradition. There is a lively pop-music scene, heavily influenced by Western styles, and the popularity of Western and Chinese movies has led to a home-based movie theater industry.

Kites and Candles

The peoples of Thailand celebrate many colorful festivals, marking religious events and temples, spirits and rituals, seasons and harvests, and the commemoration of historical events. Religious festivals are mostly dated by phases of the Moon, so they fall on different days each year.

- Chinese New Year, or Spring Festival, is the chief festival for Thailand's Chinese community, celebrated with firecrackers, dancing, and feasting.

- March sees a kite-flying festival, as winds pick up before the monsoon season. Kites have an ancient history in Thailand, and a huge variety of colorful kites take to the air.

Getting soaked to the skin during street "water battles" is all part of Songkhran, the celebrations held across the nation to mark the Thai New Year.

- April is the time for Thai New Year, or Songkhran (*sawng-KRAHN*), in which everyone hurls pails of water at each other, drenching anyone who ventures onto the streets.

- Visakha Puja (*vee-SAH-kuh POO-juh*) in May marks the Buddha's birthday. Temples celebrate with candlelit processions.

- In May the Bun Bang Thai (*BOON BAHNG TIE*) Festival is marked by the parading and firing of wooden rockets, which are said to bring on the monsoon rains.

- Loy Krathang (*LOE-ee kruh-TAHNG*), the Festival of Lights, held in October or November, is celebrated by the floating of candles and flower wreaths on rivers, lakes, and shores in order to placate the water spirits.

VIETNAM

THE NATION OF VIETNAM OCCUPIES A LONG, NARROW STRIP OF LAND along the eastern edge of the Indochina Peninsula. It measures 1,025 miles (1,650 kilometers) from north to south, but only 31 miles (50 kilometers) across at its narrowest point.

Vietnam can be divided into three separate landscape zones. The north is mostly mountainous, while central Vietnam consists of a broad inland plateau, together with the Annam Highlands. South Vietnam has rugged hills in the north, and low-lying marshy land in the southern delta region.

The far south of Vietnam is a land of rivers, canals, and marshes. There are many floating markets, reached only by boat, and also some floating houses.

Early Vietnam

The first traces of early human settlement in Vietnam (vee-EHT-NAHM) date from about 500,000 B.C.E. Archaeologists have also found remains left by hunter-gatherers who lived in Vietnam around 8000 B.C.E. By about 6000 B.C.E. these hunter-gatherers were beginning to farm small plots of land in the Red River Delta region in northern Vietnam; by 2000 B.C.E. they had learned how to grow rice. The ancestors of the present-day majority Viet people may have arrived in Vietnam around this time. They settled on the best low-lying land. This forced small groups of earlier inhabitants of Vietnam to retreat to the forests and hills.

During the next fifteen hundred years Vietnamese people learned how to make bronze. By 300 B.C.E. skilled metalworkers in northern Vietnam were making amazing *dong son* (DAWNG SAWN), or bronze

drums. In about 250 B.C.E. northern Vietnam was invaded by a Chinese warlord who founded a new kingdom called Au Lac (AHW LAHK). In 207 B.C.E. this was conquered by a rival Chinese state, Nam Viet (NAHM vee-EHT). The powerful Han emperors of China (see CHINA) conquered Nam Viet in 111 B.C.E., and the Chinese demanded tribute from northern Vietnam for the next thousand years.

Meanwhile, two new kingdoms, Funan (foo-NAHN) and Champa (CHAHM-pah), were developing in other areas of Vietnam.

FACTS AND FIGURES

Official name: *Socialist Republic of Vietnam*

Status: *Independent state*

Capital: *Hanoi*

Major towns: *Ho Chi Minh City, Haiphong, Da Nang*

Area: *130,468 square miles (337,912 square kilometers)*

Population: *81,600,000*

Population density: *625 per square mile (241 per square kilometer)*

Peoples: *88 percent Viet; 10 percent ethnic minorities (54 groups, including Tay, Hmong, Khmer, Muong, Nung, Thai); 2 percent Chinese*

Official language: *Vietnamese*

Currency: *New dong*

National day: *Independence Day (September 2)*

Country's name: Vietnam *means "land of the Viet people."*

CLIMATE

Northern Vietnam has a subtropical climate, with warm temperatures year-round. Monsoons create a wet summer season from May to September. The weather is drier between October and March. In southern Vietnam the climate is tropical, with humid weather for most of the year.

	Ho Chi Minh City	Hanoi
Average January temperature:	78°F (26°C)	63°F (17°C)
Average July temperature:	82°F (28°C)	84°F (29°C)
Average annual precipitation:	71 in. (180 cm)	72 in. (183 cm)

Time line:	First traces of early human settlement	Hunter-gatherers living in Vietnam	First rice-growing
	500,000 B.C.E.	**8000 B.C.E.**	**2000 B.C.E.**

Ruined Hindu temples at My Son, in central Vietnam. They were built of carved brick by rulers of the Champa kingdom between around 400 and 1200 C.E.

Khmer people moved to settle there; others, already living locally, were influenced by Khmer culture and customs.

People in the kingdom of Champa, in central Vietnam, lived by fishing, pottery making, rice growing, and piracy. They attacked merchant ships and fought against their neighbors. The rulers of Champa honored Hindu gods, used Sanskrit, the ancient Indian language, and built fine monuments using styles and designs from Indian art. Champa was conquered by the northern Vietnamese about 1100.

Both were influenced by the culture of India (see INDIA), the most powerful state in Southeast Asia at that time. Indian ideas were spread by merchants, scholars, and religious teachers who traveled to Vietnam.

In southern Vietnam, Funan became rich by growing rice and from trade. By the first century C.E., its farmers constructed an elaborate irrigation system. Merchants built a port called Oc-Eo (AWK-eh-YOE) in the Mekong Delta and traded with China, India, Indonesia (see INDONESIA), and Persia (modern-day Iran). They also had contact with the Mediterranean region through foreign travelers. Soon after 500 C.E., Funan was conquered by the Khmer kingdom of Chenla (CHEHN-luh), in nearby Cambodia (see CAMBODIA). Some

In northern Vietnam, Chinese conquerors gave the land a new name, *Annam* (uh-NAHM), meaning "pacified south." The Chinese introduced their own culture, based on Confucian values of respect for age and obedience and their own system of administration. The people of Vietnam rebelled several times against Chinese rule, but without success. Some of Vietnam's most famous rebels, the Trung (TROONG) sisters, set up a short-lived kingdom in 40 C.E. Chinese rule was finally overthrown in 938, when troops led by a northern Vietnamese general, Ngo Quyen, defeated the Chinese fleet.

Dai Viet Kingdom

Following the defeat of the Chinese fleet, there was fighting as other Vietnamese leaders struggled to win power. In 968

Kingdom of Au Lac founded	Chinese state Nam Viet invades northern Vietnam	Han emperors of China rule northern Vietnam
ca. 250 B.C.E.	207 B.C.E.	111 B.C.E.–938 C.E.

warrior Dinh Bo Linh took control of northern Vietnam, arranged a peace treaty with China, reorganized the army and government, and named his new kingdom Dai Viet (DIE vee-EHT), or Great Viet. Led by several dynasties of strong Buddhist rulers, Dai Viet controlled northern Vietnam for the next four hundred years. Its rulers founded a new capital on the site of modern Hanoi (ha-NOEY), built Vietnam's first university, and encouraged the spread of the Buddhist faith. They won an amazing victory in 1288, halting a threatening Mongol invasion. By 1400 Dai Viet controlled most of the same area as modern Vietnam, except for Khmer lands in the far south.

In 1407 China invaded Dai Viet, destroyed cultural treasures, captured government ministers, levied harsh taxes, and made ordinary people work as slaves. Vietnamese soldiers, led by Le Loi, fought back in 1428 and won. Until 1789, the emperors who followed Le all belonged to the ruling dynasty he founded (known as the Later Le). They tried to remove all Chinese culture from Vietnam and promoted Viet language, literature, religion, and laws.

However, Vietnam soon faced more outsiders. The first Europeans reached Vietnam in 1516, when Portuguese sailors landed in Da Nang (duh-NANG). They were followed by English and Dutch merchants, who set up trading posts, and by Christian missionaries from Portugal and France.

From about 1600 the Vietnamese kingdom was divided between two powerful rival families who ruled on behalf of the Le dynasty emperors. The Trinh (TRIHN) governed the north, while the south was controlled by the Nguyen (NOO-yehn). In 1765 three brothers in the town of Tay Son (TIE SAWN) launched a rebellion, protesting the harsh rule by the Trinh and Nguyen governors and demanding a share of the good farmland. This was mostly controlled by rich families from the ruling elite, who had close ties to the emperor or his governors. The rebels also demanded that governors rule justly and that the poorest people should not be forced to work like slaves. The rebels seized rich families' land, overthrew the Trinh and Nguyen governors, and set up their own kingdoms. Fearing for his life, the emperor asked China for help, and Chinese troops invaded. In a surprise victory they were defeated in 1789 by the Tay Son rebels, but the rebel commander died soon after, and in 1802, with French help, a Nguyen noble seized power. He proclaimed himself to be the new Vietnamese emperor and took the name Gia Long.

French Indochina

Gia Long took firm control of his kingdom, building new roads, appointing new governors, punishing the Tay Son rebels, and canceling their land reforms. He also closed the country to foreigners and persecuted missionaries. This gave the French, who were already seeking colonies in the region, an excuse to attack. After many years of fighting, they won control of the whole country in 1883. Vietnam

Dinh Bo Linh founds kingdom of Dai Viet in northern Vietnam	Dai Viet defeats Mongol invasion	China occupies Dai Viet
968 C.E.	1288	1407–1428

became part of French Indochina, controlled by the French government in the interests of France. The French allowed Gia Long's descendants to continue as emperors, but they had little real power.

French colonial rulers hoped to make money by developing Vietnam. They set up plantations to grow rice, rubber, tea, and coffee, and they built new roads and bridges. They introduced public health plans and provided some schools, but most Vietnamese people remained extremely poor. Wages on French plantations were low, working conditions were harsh, and taxes were high.

Communism and Ho Chi Minh

Opposition to French rule was led by two very different organizations. The Vietnam National Party, founded in 1927, called for the violent overthrow of the French and a new nationalist republic. In contrast, the Revolutionary Youth League, founded in 1925, wanted a communist government for Vietnam. One of its leaders, Ho Chi Minh (HOE CHEE MIHN), persuaded many different communist groups to work together against the French and supported the Nghe Tinh uprising of 1930, when twenty thousand angry workers marched on Saigon (now Ho Chi Minh City).

In 1941, during World War II (1939–1945), Vietnam was occupied by Japanese troops. The same year, Ho Chi Minh founded the Viet Minh movement to fight against them. Many Vietnamese citizens suffered during the Japanese occupation; in the north more than two

Vietnamese communist leader Nguyen That Thanh (lived 1890–1969). He was known by his supporters as Ho Chi Minh, meaning "Bringer of Bright Light."

million died from famine. The Japanese allowed the French Vichy government, which supported their ally, Nazi Germany, to continue to run the country, but when the Japanese and Vichy French were defeated in 1945, communist leader Ho Chi Minh declared Vietnam's independence. The new postwar government of France sent troops to win back control, and a bitter war broke out between the communists and the French. Fighting continued until 1954. French forces were helped with more than $3 billion in government aid from the United States. However, they could not defeat the communists, and in 1953 the United States and France both approached

Vietnam divided between Trinh and Nguyen families	Start of Tay Son rebellion	New emperor Gia Long takes control; closes country to foreigners
1600	**1765**	**1802**

the government of north Vietnam suggesting a cease-fire. The Soviet Union and China also asked north Vietnam to end the fighting. All sides agreed to start peace negotiations, but in 1954, before any truce began, French soldiers were forced to surrender by north Vietnamese communists after losing at the battle of Dien Bien Phu (DYEHN BYEHN FOO).

After the communists defeated the French, an election was planned, but nationalist leader Ngo Dinh Diem, a staunch anticommunist Roman Catholic, and his U.S. allies refused to allow it. They feared they would be defeated by the communists, so an international conference met in Geneva, Switzerland, to negotiate peace. Delegates agreed that Vietnam should be divided along the 17th parallel (line of latitude). Vietnam north of this line would become the Communist Democratic Republic of Vietnam (also called North Vietnam), with its capital at Hanoi. Land to the south would become an independent noncommunist republic, ruled by nationalists. Ho Chi Minh became president of North Vietnam. South Vietnam was ruled by Ngo Dinh Diem, who became president in 1955, when Vietnam's last emperor, Bao Dai, gave up power.

Ho Chi Minh and his supporters were not happy with this agreement. They wanted all Vietnam to be united under communist rule. They continued to campaign, and they organized guerrilla fighters to attack South Vietnam. In South Vietnam itself, the political situation became very unstable after president Ngo Dinh Diem (backed by thousands of U.S. military

advisors now stationed in Vietnam) refused to hold the elections promised at the Geneva conference, fearing the communists would win. Diem was also accused of corruption and human rights abuses. He persecuted Buddhists and forced villagers to fight against communists. In 1963 he was killed by army officers who seized power.

The Vietnam War

The new government in South Vietnam asked the United States for help to fight against communist attacks. In 1964 the United States sent troops to Vietnam to back up the military advisors already there, claiming that its ships had been attacked by communists in the Gulf of Tonkin. This was

---

The Cold War

The Vietnam War was fought against the backdrop of the Cold War, a period of tension between two superpowers: the capitalist, democratic United States and the communist Soviet Union. The Cold War began soon after the end of World War II in 1945 and ended with the collapse of the Soviet Union in the early 1990s. During the 1950s and 1960s, it was the most important issue in global politics. After 1964, Vietnam became a symbol of this tragic conflict. In the Vietnam War, communists from North Vietnam, backed by the Soviet Union, came face-to-face with U.S.-backed anticommunists from the south.

French control Vietnam	Nationalist and communist movements call for independence	Japanese occupy Vietnam
1883	**1920s–1930s**	**1941–1945**

American marines burn down a rain-forest hideout belonging to the Viet Cong (Vietnamese communist) guerrilla fighters in 1968, during the Vietnam War.

the start of the Vietnam War. By 1967 400,000 U.S. troops were fighting in Vietnam, and U.S. planes were bombing the north. Soldiers from South Korea, Thailand, Australia, and New Zealand fought alongside those from the United States. Their governments feared that communists would one day attack them. In response, the communist Soviet Union sent thousands of technical advisors to help communist fighters in the north.

At first U.S. troops had some success, but by 1968 it seemed clear that they could never win against the communist guerrillas in the countryside. United States' public opinion was shocked by the large number of U.S. casualties and by the scenes of bloodshed and suffering shown on TV.

Some people in the United States also opposed the war for ideological reasons. They thought the Vietnamese should be free to decide the future of their own country, without interference from outside.

Gradually, U.S. forces handed over the fighting to their South Vietnamese allies, although battles and bombing raids continued into the early 1970s. U.S. troops were finally withdrawn in 1973, after an agreement made at a peace conference held in Paris, France, but fighting between North and South Vietnam continued until 1975, when the north took control of all of Vietnam. In 1976 the north and south were united in a new nation. As a symbol of this victory, the South Vietnamese capital, Saigon, was renamed Ho Chi Minh City.

The Vietnam War caused great loss of life and personal suffering for soldiers and civilians on both sides. Further stresses followed after the new communist government of united Vietnam sent troops to Laos (see LAOS) to encourage communist rebels, and fought a war in Cambodia from 1975 to 1979. Vietnamese troops remained in Cambodia for the next ten years. Vietnam also became involved in border fighting with China in 1979.

In Vietnam the new government took firm steps to control its own people. Only communist political activity was allowed— all other parties were banned and democratic freedoms, such as the right to protest, were severely limited. The

War between France and Vietnamese communists	Vietnam divided into North Vietnam and South Vietnam	Vietnam War
1945–1954	**1954**	**1964–1973**

The Boat People

In the late 1970s and 1980s, thousands of small boats and homemade rafts sailed secretly away from Vietnam, carrying frightened, desperate refugees. They were heading for noncommunist Asian nations; the favorite destination was Hong Kong, then a British colony. A large number of them were members of Vietnam's Chinese ethnic minority; others came from the south and had been persecuted by Vietnam's communist rulers. About 840,000 "Boat People" reached safety and settled in their new homeland; tragically, about another forty thousand were lost at sea.

The freighter Tun An *carrying over 2,500 Vietnamese refugees, or Boat People, arriving at Manila harbor, in the Philippines, in 1979.*

communist government sent trusted officials from the north to run many southern districts. They were hostile to most southerners, even those who had opposed the South Vietnamese government before the Vietnam War. Scholars, teachers, journalists, religious leaders, and trades unionists were especially suspect. The communist government feared they might question its ideas. Many professional and business families had their property confiscated; others were sent to brutal reeducation camps.

The new government also made large-scale plans to restructure business and industry, bringing most of them under state control. It reorganized agriculture and set up Soviet-style collective farms, similar to those founded in communist Russia between the 1930s and 1950s. Collectivized Vietnamese farmers had to join their own small plots of land together and work them as a single unit, under state control. Many thousands of Vietnamese people were forcibly moved to work in government enterprises.

Years of war and political repression led many Vietnamese people to flee their

Communists control all of Vietnam	Liberal communist leader Nguyen Van Linh elected. Start of *doi moi* (economic freedom) policies.	Trade agreement with China
1975	**1986–1990**	**1991**

homeland as refugees. Some escaped via Cambodia to the United States and Europe; others risked their lives by escaping on boats, living as Boat People.

For a long time after the Vietnam War ended, the Vietnamese government shunned contact with countries friendly with the United States, but in 1986 Vietnamese communists chose a more liberal politician, Nguyen Van Linh, as their leader. They were following the example of new policies of openness and reform developed by their close ally, the Soviet Union.

Moving Forward

In 1990 Nguyen Van Linh called for *doi moi* (DOE-eh MOE-eh), or economic freedom, in Vietnam. In 1991 many new, liberal-minded members were elected to communist ruling assemblies. That same year Vietnam held friendly negotiations with its old enemy, China. It signed a treaty with the United States in 1994, ending the ban on trade between their nations.

Since then, the government's doi moi policies have encouraged massive foreign investment in Vietnam, but the government has not transformed Vietnam completely. It still has control of the economy and runs

Most Vietnamese farmers still use old-style technology to grow rice. Traditional, flat-bottom boats are used to transport harvest along shallow creeks and canals. This boat is in southern Vietnam's Mekong Delta region.

many industries. Vietnam is still a one-party state without democracy. Many governments and international organizations have strongly criticized its record on human rights.

Today, Vietnam is very poor and faces problems of pollution, a rapidly growing population, and food shortages. However, the Vietnamese people have won great admiration for their courage, determination, and hard work in rebuilding their shattered country.

The Viet People

About nine out of every ten Vietnamese belong to the Viet people, also known as the Kinh. They have lived in Vietnam for at least four thousand years, having migrated there from China about 3000 B.C.E. Settling first in the north of the country, over the centuries they came to dominate many of the other peoples living in Vietnam.

End of trade ban with United States	Vietnam signs new trade treaty with United States	New National Tourism Action Program
1994	**2001**	**2001–2002**

Traditionally the Viet people lived as rice farmers, but today they occupy the most important positions in Vietnamese society and work in a wide variety of jobs, from the traditional to the ultramodern. They also hold most government and official positions.

Viet people live in towns and cities or in lowland farming areas. In cities, they mostly occupy small houses built of wood or concrete with tiled roofs. Only the rich can afford to live in the elegant French-style mansions that survive from colonial times. In the country, many families still live in traditional two-roomed wooden homes, roofed with thatch. They also live in more modern houses, made of earth, brick, or concrete with iron roofs. Beside rivers and around the coast, many homes are raised above the ground on stilts, to prevent flooding.

Ethnic Minority Communities

About 10 percent of the Vietnamese population belongs to ethnic minority communities. There are more than fifty different peoples, each with their own traditions. They almost all live in the mountainous areas of northern and southern Vietnam. Just two groups live in the lowlands. The Cham (CHAHM) are descended from the inhabitants of Champa, in central Vietnam. The Khmer (kuh-MUHR), who live in the Mekong Delta in the south, came over from Cambodia.

Some mountain peoples, such as the Tay, Muong, and Thai, are descended from the original Malay inhabitants of Vietnam, who moved to the highland forests when new migrants arrived. Other groups, such as the Hmong, Zoa, and Nung, are descended from peoples who migrated to

These Thai ethnic minority children are wearing traditional hats. Originally from China, around one million Thai people live in the hills of northwestern Vietnam today.

Vietnam from southern China thousands of years ago.

Most ethnic minority people are farmers. Some live in settled communities, growing rice in paddies and cultivating cash crops, such as coffee. They keep animals such as water buffalo, hogs, and chickens. Others live as seminomads and farm using slash-and-burn techniques. These communities hunt wild animals in the forests and gather wild foods.

Traditionally, many ethnic peoples live in tall stilt houses, constructed of wood and bamboo. Most are for individual families only, but a few communities, such as the Ede (EH-deh), build boat-shaped longhouses to accommodate large extended family groups. In some areas traditional houses are being replaced by small, modern homes made of brick.

Most ethnic peoples still maintain their ancient customs, such as sacrificing animals to guardian spirits to bring good fortune and asking shamans (magic healers) to cure illness or communicate with spirits on their behalf. Eleven ethnic communities each have their own writing scripts. The Nung (NUHNG) people are famous for their basketry and papermaking. The Jarai (yuh-RIE) make wonderful musical instruments out of bamboo, and the Bahnar (bah-NAHR) are expert wood-carvers.

Many communities also continue to wear traditional dress, often dyed a deep blue-black using indigo, with elaborate headdresses. Hmong (MAWNG) women wear heavy silver jewelry; Dao (DOW) clothes are decorated with weaving and silver coins; the Ede people wear copper and silver jewelry, embroidered jackets, and colored beads.

Until French colonists arrived, most mountain people had little contact with lowland Vietnamese. The French cleared plantations in the mountain regions and sent in Christian missionaries, but they did not greatly interfere with traditional mountain life. After independence, governments in North and South Vietnam both aimed to integrate ethnic communities into mainstream Vietnamese society. To preserve their identity, mountain people joined together to form the United Front for the Liberation of Oppressed Races (FULRO).

In communist times the government tried again to force mountain people to give up their traditional lifestyles and sited New Economic Zones, where many lowland workers settled in ethnic community lands. Since the doi moi policy of the 1990s, however, attitudes toward ethnic people have changed. Their languages and traditions are now officially recognized, and their villages, crafts, and clothes are valued as tourist attractions. Traces of past discrimination remain, however, and most ethnic minority people are still desperately poor.

Ethnic Chinese

The population of Vietnam also includes more than a million ethnic Chinese people. Vietnamese call them the Hoa (hoe-WAH). Their ancestors migrated to Vietnam after about 1600 to work as merchants and clerks. They settled in the south of Vietnam, where most Hoa people still live.

Over the centuries Hoa people became integrated into the majority Viet community—some even worked for the Vietnamese government—but they maintained several of their ancient traditions, including their language, festivals, and schools. Most Hoa today live in cities and towns, where they run businesses, stores, and workshops. Some live in modern housing; others occupy

People from the Muong ethnic minority live in the hill country close to Hanoi, in northern Vietnam. They use water buffalo to cultivate flooded paddies, where they grow rice.

traditional long and narrow merchant houses in busy shopping streets.

Hoa people were badly persecuted in the years after 1975, when an anti-Chinese government ruled Vietnam. Many fled as refugees. Hoa people who remained in Vietnam are now accepted as members of society, valued for their business experience and language skills.

The Vietnamese Language

The official language of Vietnam is Vietnamese, also called Kinh (KIHN). No one knows its origins, but experts think it probably developed from a mixture of Thai, Chinese, and Khmer, all used in nearby lands. It is spoken using six different tones; the meaning of each word depends on the tone a speaker uses.

An inscription from the Imperial Palace in the city of Hue, built early in the nineteenth century. This inscription is carved in Chinese characters.

For example, the word *ma* (MAH) can mean mother, ghost, horse, and more.

Until about 1300, Vietnamese was written using Chinese characters called *chu nho* (CHOO NOE). Then Vietnamese scholars invented their own way of writing, called *chu nom* (CHOO NOEM). Today, Vietnamese is written in a script based on the Roman alphabet, called *quoc ngu* (KWAWK NYOO). This was invented by a French priest in the seventeenth century, to help him write Christian texts in Vietnamese.

There are three main dialects of modern Vietnamese, spoken in the north, south, and central regions. They all contain similar words but are pronounced so differently that speakers from different parts of the country often cannot understand each other.

The ethnic minority peoples of Vietnam all speak their own languages and dialects. Some minority languages are spoken quite widely throughout the mountain regions. Others are understood by just a few hundred people and are in danger of being lost forever.

Let's Talk Vietnamese

Xin chao *(SHIHN CHAH-oe)*	Hello
Toi khoe cam on *(TWAH KHOE kahm AWN)*	Pleased to meet you
Ten la gi? *(TEHN lah JEE)*	What is your name?
Ten toi la . . . *(TEHN TWAH LAH)*	My name is . . .
Ong [or ba, if talking to a woman] co the giup toi khong? *(AWNG co tae gee-OOP twah KAWNG)*	Can you help me?
Xin loi *(SHIN LOE-ee)*	Excuse me
Lam on *(LAHM AWN)*	Please
Cam on nhieu *(KAM AWN NYOO)*	Thank you

573

While Vietnam was ruled by France, the French language was used for all government business and by educated Vietnamese people. Some older Vietnamese men and women still speak it, but it is not widely used. In the same way, Russian was spoken by keen communists in Vietnam from about 1950 to 1990. Now that Vietnamese government policies have changed, it is falling out of use.

Today the most popular second language in Vietnam is English. Many Vietnamese soldiers and civilians, especially in the south, learned it during wartime from U.S. troops.

Members of the Hoa ethnic minority in southern Vietnam still speak Chinese. The number of people studying to learn Chinese is growing throughout Vietnam as contacts with nearby Chinese-speaking countries, such as Taiwan, become more important.

Religion

During communist rule, the Vietnamese government disapproved of religion and tried to ban it. Many monks and priests were cruelly treated, and religious buildings were damaged. Since the 1990s, however, religious activity has been tolerated, and Vietnam has seen a religious revival.

Today, Vietnamese people follow four major religious traditions: Buddhism, Confucianism, Taoism, and Christianity. They often select different elements from these faiths to suit needs in their lives. For example, they might ask Buddhist monks to perform a funeral ceremony, make offerings to their ancestors using Confucian

The Tet Festival

For most Vietnamese people, the Tet Festival, marking the start of the Lunar New Year, is the most important holiday. Families meet to celebrate, and ancestral spirits are believed to join them. People say that household spirits, sometimes called **Ong Tao** *(AWNG TAHW: the Kitchen God), go to heaven to report on past year's events. To symbolize this, people release live fish into rivers and leave offerings of food for the spirits' journeys. They also settle debts, clear unfinished business, give presents, prepare special food, such as* banh chung *(BAHN CHOONG), pies of pork and beans, and clean their houses and ancestors' graves.*

The fierce head of a spectacular dragon costume, worn by a dancer at the Tet (New Year) Festival in Ho Chi Minh City in southern Vietnam.

rituals, and consult a Taoist fortune-teller before setting out on a journey.

Traditionally, Vietnamese people followed the Mahayana branch of Buddhism. This teaches that each individual should strive for perfect, virtuous behavior. Followers worship Buddhas and bodhisattvas—spirits who have lived good lives but stay on earth to help others. They say prayers, make offerings at temples, and consult monks for spiritual guidance.

Confucian philosophy has shaped Vietnamese attitudes to their rulers and also relations within the family. Children are taught to honor the spirits of their ancestors, especially on the anniversary of their deaths. Many Vietnamese homes have a family altar where offerings are made to ancestor spirits. Families also display memorial plaques and photos of dead relatives in beautiful pagodas.

Taoism originated as a philosophy, a way of understanding the world rather than as a religion, but in Vietnam its followers developed many rituals that include magic, fortune-telling, and astrology. They honor many different gods and immortals. Some Taoist believers act as mediums, as they communicate between living worshipers and the spirit world.

Christianity was brought to Vietnam by Roman Catholic missionaries, and there are now about eight million Catholics in Vietnam. They are free to worship, but the state controls the appointment of priests and monitors Catholic activities, such as teaching. During the twentieth century, U.S. Protestants preached an evangelical variety of Christianity, and there are now about 400,000 Protestants in Vietnam.

Members of the Khmer and Cham minorities are Muslims. They follow a simple form of Islam, praying only once a week on Friday and often drinking alcohol, which is usually forbidden for Muslims. Some Muslims also make offerings to Hindu holy statues that still survive in Vietnam. In Ho Chi Minh City, Khmer and Cham people worship at Hindu temples.

Whatever faith they follow, many Vietnamese people still hold animist beliefs. These include ancestor worship and faith in the power of spirits living around them. Communities also worship their own special guardian spirits, which may be magical creatures or dead heroes.

Two new religions originated in Vietnam. *Cao Dai* (KAHW DIE), or "high place," was first preached in the 1920s. It blends teachings from all the world's great

Crowds of worshipers attend a Cao Dai religious service in Tay Ninh province. At Cao Dai temples priests make offerings of incense, tea, fruit, and flowers four times a day.

Phong Thuy

Many Vietnamese consult practitioners of phong thuy *(FAWNG THOOY: a system similar to Chinese feng shui) before making important decisions or starting on any building project. They believe that invisible forces run through the environment and that invisible spirits live there. If forces are disturbed or spirits are offended by changes in their surroundings, they can cause unhappiness or bad luck. It is especially unfortunate to site ancestors' tombs incorrectly. Followers believe that if their spirits cannot rest they will trouble their living descendants. Starting work on an unlucky date can also cause problems. Troubled businesspeople also ask phong thuy experts for advice on how to increase their profits, for example, by moving doors and windows, making offerings to temples, or moving ancestors' tombs.*

nationalist politics and were treated as dangerous revolutionaries by the French, the nationalist government, and the communists. Today there are probably more than a million believers in Hoa Hao in Vietnam, and they are still treated with suspicion by the government.

Society

During the twentieth century Vietnamese people lived through many dramatic changes. Each new government had different social policies. However, many traditional values still shape Vietnamese society today.

The family still plays the most important part in Vietnamese peoples' lives. Children are taught to respect older people and to put the needs of the family group before their own individual desires. Politeness

Young women in Hanoi, in northern Vietnam, wearing traditional costume: a close-fitting tunic with long panels in the front and back, worn over loose black or white pants.

religions into one "super-faith." Followers are encouraged to lead pure and honest lives, to meditate, and pray four times a day. They honor the Supreme Being and many saints. Worship at Cao Dai temples is led by nine different grades of priest, who wear specially colored robes. There are also mediums, who hold séances. Cao Dai has about two million followers in Vietnam and thousands more among Vietnamese living overseas.

Hoa Hao (hoe-WAH HAH-oe), or "peace and kindness," originated as a Buddhist sect in the 1930s. It was founded by a monk, Huynh Phu So, who wanted to purify Buddhist ways of worship. Its members soon became involved in

Workers and shoppers in Ho Chi Minh City board ferries to take them home. Other favorite forms of transportation in the city include buses, rickshaws, and bicycles.

and self control are highly valued, as is maintaining individual dignity and family prestige in dealings with others. It is seen as great misfortune not to be married.

According to Vietnamese law, women have equal opportunities with men, and there are many well-educated Vietnamese women. In cities some have high-status professional careers, but in the countryside many women still follow traditional lives as homemakers, caring for the family and working very hard in farms and on paddies.

Traditional Vietnamese ideas about modest dress and social customs, such as bowing or shaking hands on meeting, are still widespread. Most Vietnamese think it is a duty to be gracious and hospitable to guests and visitors; all believe in the value of determined hard work without complaining.

Because of Vietnam's troubled history, it is perhaps not surprising that the suspicion and hostility between what were North and South Vietnam still remain. In recent years this has been made worse by the growing gap between the very rich and the very poor. Most new developments are based in the south, and southern cities, especially Ho Chi Minh City, now have glittering new and expensive business districts, with stylish stores, apartment buildings, and hotels. Outside the cities, especially in the north, most Vietnamese people live in poor conditions in the countryside.

Fast, new city developments have brought riches to some businesspeople, but they have also led to serious social problems, such as rising levels of crime, drug abuse, and prostitution. There are also growing numbers of beggars and street children.

Economy

Vietnam is one of the poorest countries in Asia. Almost 40 percent of the population lives below the poverty line. The richest 10 percent of the population consumes almost a third of the national wealth; the poorest 10 percent has only 3 percent of it. This poverty is made worse by a serious unemployment problem. One in four Vietnamese workers cannot find a job.

Doi Moi (Economic Freedom)

In the early 1990s the government encouraged people to set up small businesses. Foreign firms built new offices and factories to produce modern consumer goods. In 1994 they were joined by U.S. multinational companies. For a while the economy boomed, although rapid growth led to problems of exploitation and environmental damage. Many people complained that traditional values were being traded for foreign ideas, and advertisements and business signs in English were torn down. Thousands of country families moved to crowded towns, hoping, but often failing, to find work. Those who stayed in the countryside received few benefits from new economic developments.

The economic boom caused by doi moi was halted in 1997 by the Asian financial crisis. Many companies collapsed, leaving workers with no jobs and no income. Some foreign investors left Vietnam altogether. Since this crisis, Vietnam's economy is starting to grow once again, partly due to development projects funded by overseas aid. New roads, bridges, and government offices have been built and new regional markets opened. A new industrial zone has been set up in the province of Binh Duong (BIHN DWAWNG) in the south of the country.

Aid donors have forced the Vietnamese government to reform its economic policies. They have also introduced plans to invest in information technology and expand the tourist industry. In 2001 Vietnam signed a new trade treaty with the United States. It also made agreements with Great Britain and Japan to exploit reserves of oil and gas off the coast.

Today Vietnam's chief industries are food processing; clothing and shoe manufacture; machine making; coal and iron-ore mining; cement, steel, and fertilizer production; and making glass, vehicle tires, and paper. Together with service industries, which include tourism, catering, transportation, and entertainment, they employ about one-third of all working people.

The remaining two-thirds of the Vietnamese workforce are farmers. In the north they work on cooperative farms, set up during the communist years. In the south some own small plots of land. Many men and women also work as laborers on large plantations. Farmers grow food to feed their families but also have to follow government instructions about which crops to grow for export overseas. Vietnam's main farm products are rice, corn, potatoes, soybeans, coffee, tea, bananas, sugar, poultry, and hogs—and also rubber, produced from the sap of tropical trees.

Vietnam's national forest management policy has achieved positive results. It is the only country in eastern Asia to have increased its area of tropical rain forest, by banning the export of all unprocessed timber in 1992. Today there are 10 percent more trees in Vietnam than there were in 1995, and there are many reforestation

A massive truck, loaded with felled tree trunks from the rain forest, lumbers past a traditional bullock cart carrying tree saplings for replanting.

plans. There are also plans to protect the countryside and create jobs there by attracting tourists to new national parks.

Food

Vietnamese meals are based on fresh local products—rice, vegetables, herbs, and fruit—together with fish caught in rivers and around the coast. Vietnamese people also eat other wild creatures, such as bats, deer, crabs, snakes, and frogs. For special occasions, dog meat is popular. Traditionally they believe that eating certain creatures will improve their health or give them special powers. Eating snake, for example, is said to make diners strong, and snake heart in wine is believed to be a love potion.

The main ingredient in most Vietnamese meals is

These workers in a silk factory at Bao Lac, northern Vietnam, have met to share their lunchtime meal during a welcomed break.

rice, with small amounts of meat and vegetables. For extra taste, diners add salty, strong-smelling *nuoc mam* (nuh-WAWK MAM), a sauce made from fermented fish, sometimes flavored with lime, chili, and garlic. Sugar is added to many savory dishes as a seasoning.

Most Vietnamese homes do not have an oven. Cooks use gas burners to cook rice and fried dishes. People like to join their family or friends for meals, so several dishes are usually served together for diners to share. Food is eaten with chopsticks, and soup is sipped from ceramic spoons. Vietnamese people usually get up very early. Breakfast is eaten between 5 and 6 a.m., lunch between 11:30 a.m. and 1:30 p.m., and the main evening meal about 5 p.m.

Many Vietnamese start their day with *pho* (FOE), rice noodles in a thin, clear broth, made from bones and flavored with ginger, coriander, spring onions, or other herbs. Wealthy families add shreds of pork or

chicken. At other times of the day, popular dishes include *com tay cam* (KAWM TIE KAHM), rice with mushrooms, chicken, and ginger; *bun cha* (BOON CHAH), noodles with pork, vegetables, chili, sugar, and vinegar; *cha que* (CHAH KAE), grilled fish with cinnamon; and *nem* (NEHM), or spring rolls. These are thin rice-flour pancakes wrapped around chopped pork, shrimp, or crab, mixed with bean sprouts, onions,

---

Pho (Noodle Soup)

You will need:

1 beef stock cube
4½ cups (1 liter) water
1 onion, finely chopped
3 tsp (15 milliliters) cooking oil
small piece fresh ginger, peeled and chopped
5 black peppercorns, crushed, or freshly ground black pepper
7 oz (200 grams) fine rice noodles
2 tsp (10 milliliters) fish sauce
3 tsp (15 grams) chopped basil, mint, or coriander leaves
3 tsp (15 grams) chopped, cleaned spring onions

Dissolve stock cube in water. Heat to boiling point. Fry onion in oil until soft. Add ginger and pepper to onion. Fry gently for 2 to 3 minutes. Add to stock.

Heat stock to boiling point. Simmer for 5 minutes. Add rice noodles to boiling stock. Let them cook for about 4 to 8 minutes, according to directions on packet. Add fish sauce; chopped basil, mint, or coriander; and spring onions. Stir well and serve.

This quantity serves four people.

---

edible fungus, and rice noodles, and then fried. They are served with fresh lettuce or mint leaves and dipped in fish sauce.

Buddhist monks and nuns are vegetarians, and, for religious reasons, many other Vietnamese people do not eat meat at times of the full moon and the new moon. Poor families cannot afford to eat meat as often as they may like. Vegetarian dishes include *com xao thap cam* (KAWM SHAHW THAHP KAHM), fried rice and vegetables, and *tau hu kho* (TAHW HOO KOE), braised soybean curd.

In cities and towns there are many stores selling French-style bread and cakes, and stalls offering quick meals and take-out snacks. Dishes served include fried rice, soups, fish, pickles, and eggs. For wealthy diners there are elegant restaurants serving dishes once cooked for the emperor's court, such as *banh nan* (BAHN NAHN), delicate ground pork, shrimp, and rice flour, steamed in banana leaves, and also French haute cuisine.

For dessert Vietnamese people eat fresh local fruit such as custard apples, lychees, papayas, special green bananas, and coconuts. Seasonal treats include the durian fruit (which smells foul but tastes good) and the dragon fruit. This is large and bright purple, with juicy and sweet white flesh and black seeds. Ice cream, U.S.-style, is sold in most towns, and street vendors serve crisp, sweet banana fritters.

Tea and coffee are both grown in Vietnam. Green tea, served weak and without milk or sugar, accompanies most meals. It is offered to guests arriving at Vietnamese homes and to customers at business meetings. Coffee, served black, sweet, and extremely strong is usually drunk in between meals, with cakes or pastries, or after dinner. Occasionally it is mixed with condensed milk to make a thick, syrupy dessert.

Many different kinds of beer are brewed in Vietnam and sold to local people and to customers overseas. Neighborhood deliveries are often made by motorcycle.

Vietnamese bars and stalls sell cool, refreshing beverages such as fresh fruit juice, mineral water, and soda. Local cold beverages include *nuoc dua* (NWAHK doo-WAH), or coconut milk, and the juice from crushed sugarcane. Breweries in Vietnam produce many different kinds of beer, while mountain vineyards produce wine.

Health Care

Medical services were severely disrupted during the Vietnam War. Many people were injured in the fighting, and others suffered when their surroundings were sprayed with chemical defoliants. Since the war ended, Vietnamese governments have tried to improve health care. In cities and big towns there are hospitals staffed by trained doctors and nurses. In country villages there are first-aid posts and maternity clinics.

The government has also run public health-education programs such as the Three Cleans Movement, which raises standards of hygiene in food preparation, housing, and water supplies, and the Three Exterminations Movement, which helps kill rats, mosquitoes, and flies. Recently the government has introduced a "Two-Child Family" policy, which aims to stop Vietnam's population from increasing; a large population places additional pressure on health care and food supplies.

Corruption, rigid bureaucracy, and shortage of money mean that some plans have not been successful. Many health clinics, especially in country districts, are poorly equipped and can do little to help the seriously ill. One child in every twenty still dies before he or she reaches five years old.

Malaria and dengue fever, both spread by mosquitoes, cause many deaths in Vietnam, as do diseases carried by polluted water, such as typhoid and cholera. Tuberculosis, caused by bacteria that breed in damp, crowded living conditions, is a serious problem. Poisonous marine life, such as jellyfish, stonefish, and sea snakes, live around the coast.

Vietnam is close to the golden triangle area of Thailand and Laos, where opium (used to make the drug heroin) and cannabis (a drug produced from the hemp plant) are grown. Drug use in Vietnam causes serious health problems and contributes to the increase in HIV/AIDS. More than forty thousand Vietnamese men,

Traditional Medicine

Many Vietnamese people still choose to rely on traditional healers who use a number of different techniques. Some are local; others have reached Vietnam from China. Traditional Vietnamese treatments include cao gio *(KAHW JYOE), in which the skin is rubbed with herbal oils and then scraped, and* giac hoi *(GYAHK HOEY), in which little pieces of burning cotton are placed inside cups of bamboo and glass and held against the patient's body. Both processes are believed to release "poisonous wind" that is traditionally thought to cause disease. Chinese medical treatments include acupuncture and herbal medicine.*

This traditional healer, from the Dao ethnic minority community in northwestern Vietnam, offers his patients giac hoi treatments to help release "poisonous wind."

women, and children have also been killed or injured by mines and bombs left behind at the end of the Vietnam War. Some experts think that wartime chemical pollution remains a grave health hazard.

Today a young girl from the Viet or Hoa communities can expect to live until she is seventy-three years old, and a boy until he is sixty-eight years. However, members of many ethnic minority groups have shorter life expectancy, chiefly because of poverty.

Education

Traditional Confucian philosophy, along with more modern ideas such as personal ambition and competitiveness, contributes to a highly valued education system in Vietnamese society. About 94 percent of the adult population can read and write. This figure is higher in towns but lower in mountain areas, where members of ethnic minority groups have, until recently, had few opportunities to attend school.

Education is provided by the state and by new schools that charge high fees. It is compulsory between the ages of six and twelve. Students spend this time at elementary schools and junior high schools. After that they can progress to three years of high school, and, if they are very fortunate, go on to college. Vietnam does not have enough places at colleges for all students who wish to attend, and most young people need to work to survive, so they cannot go. The brightest and most determined apply for a limited number of government scholarships, which pay for their living expenses and tuition fees.

Until recently, all public-school students had to spend some time learning practical skills to help rebuild their country. They still take part in ecological projects such as planting trees. Today the government tries to encourage education in technology, business, and engineering, but the most prestigious and popular courses are those that teach traditional subjects such as law and medicine.

Entertainment, Sports, and Arts

Vietnam has a long history of music making, and today music remains the most popular form of entertainment. Musical styles vary from traditional *hat cheo* (HAHT cheh-OE), or popular theater, and performances played on ancient instruments such as the *dan bau* (DAHN BAHW), a one-string fiddle, to modernized versions of folk music played by classically trained musicians. Karaoke and electronic rock are also popular. In recent years performances by ethnic minority musicians, performing in authentic style, have also become popular. They specialize in musical techniques such as alternate singing, in which pairs or groups of singers perform alternate verses. Many ethnic communities also have their own dance traditions.

Other popular traditional entertainments include *roi nuoc* (ROEY NWAWK), or water puppetry, in which huge wooden puppets on long poles act out acrobatic movements and retell ancient legends, while appearing to dance on the surface of a river or lake. Their operators stand in the water, hidden behind a bamboo screen.

The ancient martial art of thai *cuc quyen* (KUHK KOO-yehn), or shadow boxing, is Vietnam's most popular sport. In many places crowds gather in open spaces at sunrise to practice its slow, graceful movements, which are believed to increase strength and agility. Among wealthy Vietnamese, golf is a favorite game and also a status symbol.

Traditional Vietnamese arts include sculpture, used on temples and tombs; lacquerware, often inlaid with mother-of-pearl; ceramics; and painting on silk. These still exist, but the most popular modern art form is movies. Vietnamese moviemakers, such as Tran Anh Hung, have won international acclaim for their work. His first success, *The Scent of Green Papaya*, is moving and poetic, but his more recent films, such as *Cyclo*, are dramatic and sometimes shocking.

Dramatic, decorative masks made for water puppets are offered for sale to tourists in Hanoi as souvenirs of their visit to Vietnam.

Glossary

archaeology the scientific study of ancient cultures through the examination of their material remains, such as fossil relics, monuments, and tools.

bodhisattva a spirit who has lived a good life but stays on earth to help others.

Cold War name given to the hostility that existed between the free enterprise capitalist and the communist worlds between 1947 and the late 1980s.

colony a country or area that is ruled by another country.

communist a believer in communism, a theory that suggests that all property belongs to the community and that work should be organized for the common good.

democracy a state ruled by the people; a state in which government is carried out by representatives elected by the public.

doi moi economic freedom.

exile somebody who is forced to live in another country for personal or political reasons.

guerrilla a member of an irregular fighting force whose tactics include ambushes, surprise attacks, and sabotage rather than intense, close battles with the enemy.

head-hunting the practice of cutting off the heads of enemies killed in battle and preserving them as trophies.

hub the most important or active part of a place.

hunter-gatherer somebody who lives by no other means than hunting and gathering.

immigrate to leave a country or region to go and live elsewhere.

irrigate to supply land with water brought through pipes or ditches.

lacquer a coating, such as a varnish, that dries quickly into a shiny layer.

migrant somebody who moves from one place to another in search of work or economic opportunities.

monk a member of a religious community made up of men who devote themselves to prayer, solitude, and contemplation.

monsoon a wind in the Indian Ocean and southern Asia that blows from the southwest from April to October and from the northeast from October to April.

mosque a Muslim place of worship.

nationalism a loyalty or devotion to a country; the promotion of policies designed to benefit and support a particular nation.

Nazi a member of the German National Socialist Party that came to power in 1933 under the leadership of Adolf Hitler.

paddy a field in which rice is grown.

peninsula a piece of land sticking out from the mainland into a sea or lake.

plateau a broad, flat area of high land.

province a division of a country having its own government.

Resistance an illegal secret organization that fights for freedom against an occupying power.

sorghum a cereal plant widely cultivated in tropical areas as a grain crop and for animal feed.

strait a narrow body of water that joins two larger bodies of water.

totem an object revered as a symbol of a group and often used in rituals.

United Nations an alliance founded in 1945 that today includes most of the countries in the world. Its aim is to encourage international cooperation and peace.

Vietnam War a conflict in which the communist forces of North Vietnam and guerrillas in South Vietnam fought against the non-Communist forces of South Vietnam and the United States.

World War I a conflict that broke out in Europe in 1914. The Entente powers, or Allies, (which included the United Kingdom, France, and Russia) fought the Central Powers (which included Austria-Hungary, Germany, and Turkey). The United States joined the Allies in 1917. The war ended in 1918.

World War II a war that began in Europe in 1939 and spread to involve many other countries worldwide. It ended in 1945. The United Kingdom, France, the Soviet Union, the United States, Canada, Australia, New Zealand, and other European countries fought against Germany, Italy, and Japan.

Further Reading

Internet Sites

Look under Countries A to Z in the Atlapedia Online Web Site at
http://www.atlapedia.com

Use the drop-down menu to select a country on the CIA World Factbook Web Site at
http://www.odci.gov/cia/publications/factbook

Browse the Table of Contents in the Library of Congress Country Studies Web Site at
http://lcweb2.loc.gov/frd/cs/cshome.html

Use the Country Locator Maps in the World Atlas Web Site at
http://www.worldatlas.com/aatlas/world.htm

Look under the alphabetical country listing using the Infoplease Atlas at
http://www.infoplease.com/countries.html

Use the drop-down menu to select a country using E-Conflict™ World Encyclopedia at
http://www.emulateme.com

Look under the alphabetical country listing in the Yahooligans Around the World Directory at
http://www.yahooligans.com/Around_the_World/Countries

Choose the part of the world you're interested in, then scroll down to choose the country using the Geographia Web Site at
http://www.geographia.com

Taiwan

Green, Robert. *Taiwan (Modern Nations of the World).* San Diego, CA: Lucent Books, 2001.

Ryan, Michaela. *Taiwan (Countries of the World).* Milwaukee, WI: Gareth Stevens, 2003.

Salter, Christopher. *Taiwan (Modern World Nations).* Philadelphia, PA: Chelsea House Publishers, 2004.

Wee, Jesse. *Taiwan.* Philadelphia, PA: Chelsea House Publishers, 1998.

Thailand

Boraas, Tracey. *Thailand.* Mankato, MN: Bridgestone Books, 2002.

Campbell, Geoffrey A. *Thailand (Modern Nations of the World).* San Diego, CA: Lucent Books, 2000.

Cherry, Ronald. *Thailand (Countries of the World).* Milwaukee, WI: Gareth Stevens, 2000.

Ericson, Alex. *Thailand (Countries: Faces and Places).* Chanhassen, MN: Child's World, 2001.

Guile, Melanie. *Thailand.* Austin, TX: Raintree Steck-Vaughn, 2004.

Hill, Valerie. *Thailand.* Broomall, PA: Mason Crest Publishers, 2003.

Petersen, David. *Thailand.* New York: Children's Press, 2001.

Wilkins, Frances. *Thailand (Major World Nations).* Philadelphia, PA: Chelsea House, 2000.

Vietnam

Condra-Peters, Amy, and Karen Kwek. *Vietnam (Countries of the World).* Milwaukee, WI: Gareth Stevens, 2002.

Gray, Shirley Wimbish. *Vietnam (True Book).* New York: Children's Press, 2003.

Kalman, Bobbie. *Vietnam – The People (Lands, Peoples, and Cultures).* New York: Crabtree Publishers, 2002.

Merrick, Patrick. *Vietnam (Countries: Faces and Places).* Chanhassen, MN: Child's World, 2000.

Simpson, Judith. *Vietnam.* Broomall, PA: Mason Crest Publishers, 2003.

Index

Page numbers in *italic* indicate illustrations.

Page numbers in *italic* indicate illustrations.